# Thomas Jefferson and Maria Cosway: A Gordian Love Affair

Complete Correspondence with Critical Commentary

M. Andrew Holowchak

Series in American History

Copyright © 2024 Vernon Press, an imprint of Vernon Art and Science Inc, on behalf of the author.

All rights reserved. No part of this publication may be reproduced, stored in a retrieval system, or transmitted in any form or by any means, electronic, mechanical, photocopying, recording, or otherwise, without the prior permission of Vernon Art and Science Inc.

www.vernonpress.com

| In the Americas: | In the rest of the world: |
|---|---|
| Vernon Press | Vernon Press |
| 1000 N West Street, Suite 1200 | C/Sancti Espiritu 17, |
| Wilmington, Delaware, 19801 | Malaga, 29006 |
| United States | Spain |

Series in American History

Library of Congress Control Number: 2023950111

ISBN: 979-8-8819-0067-0

Also available: 978-1-64889-815-0 [Hardback]; 978-1-64889-863-1 [PDF, E-Book]

Product and company names mentioned in this work are the trademarks of their respective owners. While every care has been taken in preparing this work, neither the authors nor Vernon Art and Science Inc. may be held responsible for any loss or damage caused or alleged to be caused directly or indirectly by the information contained in it.

Cover design by Vernon Press with elements from Freepik.

Thomas Jefferson: Jefferson Portrait by John Trumbull (Painting) owned by Monticello, Thomas Jefferson Foundation (Public domain). https://www.monticello.org/research-education/thomas-jefferson-encyclopedia/jefferson-portrait-john-trumbull-painting/

Maria Cosway: Richard Cosway - Retrato de Mrs. Cosway (Public domain). https://en.m.wikipedia.org/wiki/File:Richard_Cosway_-_Retrato_de_Mrs._Cosway.JPG

Every effort has been made to trace all copyright holders, but if any have been inadvertently overlooked the publisher will be pleased to include any necessary credits in any subsequent reprint or edition.

For Monica, who made this book possible.

# Table of Contents

| | | |
|---|---|---|
| | *List of Figures* | vii |
| | *Preface* | ix |
| | *Introduction* | xiii |
| Chapter I | **The Year 1786** | 1 |
| Chapter II | **The Year 1787** | 31 |
| Chapter III | **The Year 1788** | 49 |
| Chapter IV | **The Year 1789** | 65 |
| Chapter V | **The Years 1790 to 1805** | 75 |
| Chapter VI | **The Years 1819 to 1824** | 99 |
| | *Postscript* | 113 |

# List of Figures

| | | |
|---|---|---|
| **Figure I-1:** | John Trumbull's Self-Portrait, c. 1802 | xiv |
| **Figure I-2:** | John Trumbull, *Declaration of Independence*, 1819 | xvii |
| **Figure I-3:** | John Trumbull, *Miniature of Jefferson*, 1788 | xvii |
| **Figure I-4:** | Maria Cosway, *Self-Portrait*, 1778 | xviii |
| **Figure I-5:** | Thomas Patch, *Charles Hadfield*, n.d. | xix |
| **Figure I-6:** | Thomas Patch, *Punch Party in Florence*, 1760. | xx |
| **Figure I-7:** | Violante Cerrotti, *Self-Portrait*, n.d. | xxiv |
| **Figure I-8:** | Johann Zoffany, *La Tribuna*, 1772–1778. | xxv |
| **Figure I-9:** | Joshua Reynold, *Self-Portrait*, 1775 | xxvi |
| **Figure I-10:** | Maria Kauffmann, *Self-Portrait*, c. 1773 | xxxi |
| **Figure I-11:** | Richard Cosway, Self-portrait in charcoal with water coloring, n.d. | xxxiii |
| **Figure I-12:** | Richard Cosway, *George, the Prince of Wales*, c. 1781 | xxxv |
| **Figure I-13:** | Maria Cosway, *Georgiana Cavendish*, 1782 | xxxviii |
| **Figure I-14:** | Maria Cosway, *Creusa Appearing to Aeneas*, 1781 | xxxix |
| **Figure I-15:** | Francesco Barolozzi, *Maria Costive*, 1786 | xli |
| **Figure I-16:** | Shomberg House. c. 1850 | xlii |
| **Figure 1-1:** | Nicolas-Marie-Joseph Chapuy, Halle aux Blés, 1838 | 8 |
| **Figure 2-1:** | Maria Cosway, *Young Bacchus*, 1787 | 42 |
| **Figure 3-1:** | Francesco Bartolozzi, *Engraving of Cosway's painting*, 1788 | 59 |
| **Figure 4-1:** | John Henry Hintermeister, *Foundation of American Government*, 1925 | 70 |
| **Figure 5-1:** | Richard Cosway, Portrait of Luigi Marchesi, 1790 | 79 |
| **Figure 5-2:** | John Trumbull, *Miniature of Jefferson*, 1788 | 89 |
| **Figure 5-3:** | Richard Cosway, Louisa Paolina Cosway on Her Deathbed, 1796 | 92 |
| **Figure 5-4:** | Cardinal Joseph Fesch, n.d. | 96 |
| **Figure 6-1:** | C. Bohn, *University of Virginia*, 1856 | 100 |

# Preface

Every biographer of Jefferson, at some point, has to grapple with Thomas Jefferson's relationship with Maria Cosway. Almost all biographers focus on Jefferson's celebrated, perhaps infamously so, *billet doux* of October 12, 1786—an inordinately lengthy letter, written wholly with Jefferson's left hand because of a fractured right wrist and, in my estimation, the most incredible letter of the thousands of letters he has penned. In that letter, a love-struck Jefferson, despondent after Cosway's departure from Paris *en route* to London, struggles to express his feelings for her. His struggle takes the form of a debate of sorts between his rational and moral faculties, housing respectively reason, the faculty of intellect, and feeling, the faculty of the moral sense. Scholars typically focus on the nature of that debate and wrangle among themselves about whether Head or Heart wins the debate, and I note that there is no scholarly consensus on the winner. All at some point state the obvious: that the relationship does not eventuate successfully.

Yet among the very many who note the genuineness of feelings between the two—there are strangely a few scholars like Onuf who acknowledge merely friendly flirtation and nothing more—almost all admit reciprocity of affection. The intense and overwhelming feelings that Jefferson clumsily expresses for Cosway in his *billet doux* are also felt, though perhaps less overwhelmingly, by Cosway. Her many pouty letters on their separation—while Jefferson is in Paris and Cosway is in London—are, they argue, evidence of reciprocity.[1] That, of course, makes for a more attractive and marketable narrative, but that hypothesis is untenable. Poutiness was part of Cosway's personality, and she often used it to large effect whenever she was aware of someone having interest in her.

Scrutiny of the letters between the two does not evince reciprocity of feeling. While Jefferson, in his ham-fisted manner, somewhat unreservedly expresses his love for Cosway in his *billet doux*, a careful examination of their letters shortly thereafter shows that she does not share the depth and intensity of Jefferson's feelings. I find it incredible how that is missed by most scholars. To set that record straight is a large motivation for this book.

---

[1] E.g., John Kaminski, *Jefferson in Love: The Love Letters between Thomas Jefferson & Maria Cosway* (Lanham, MD: Rowman & Littlefield, 1999), 22–23, and George Green Shackelford, *Thomas Jefferson's Travels in Europe, 1784–1789* (Baltimore: Johns Hopkins University Press, 1995), 65–74.

A second motivation for this book is that there has never been a collection of all the letters of Jefferson and Cosway. John Kaminski, in 2001, has an edition that has the letters between the two till 1790, but he, unfortunately, ends there, and there is, I show in this edition, more to their story that needs to be said, and that "more" can only be unpacked by examination of their late-in-life letters.

Other than significant biographies of Jefferson, there are several important books that have a bearing on the Jefferson-Cosway relationship.

Helen Duprey Bullock wrote *My Head and My Heart: A Little History of Thomas Jefferson and Maria Cosway* in 1945. The motivation for her "little history" is the recent acquisition of 25 missing letters of the Jefferson-Cosway correspondence. She is an advocate of reciprocated love.

There is also, as I have already mentioned, John Kaminski's collection of their love letters: *Jefferson in Love*. He ends his collection in 1790, I suppose because the ardor between the two morphs into affectionate amicability. Yet during that time, the letters show "deep and passionate love" that may have been consummated.[2] Ending the collection in 1790 is, I argue, a mistake. While Jefferson's feelings for Cosway are immediate and intense upon their first meeting and while those feelings slowly abate over time, it is very probable that Cosway, late in her life, when she is without her husband and when she is relegated to her school for girls in Lodi, comes to love Jefferson in a manner that she before could never have imagined. If that is so—and I argue that it is, and that is a third incentive for this book—then it is necessary to include the entirety of their correspondence.

The most significant book on the affair is Carol Burnell's *Divided Affections: The Extraordinary Life of Maria Cosway: Celebrity Artist and Thomas Jefferson's Impossible Love*. The book is "dramatized with conversations" for improved narrative flow, though historical purists, of whom I am one, might find that objectionable. Still, it is meticulously researched, and thus, it is invaluable to those wanting to gain access to the mind and life of Maria Cosway. That, however, proves to be a second defect of the book. Because it is so meticulously researched, it would have been better crafted as a scholarly book without the defect of hyper-concern for narrative flow through fictive conversations. A third defect, also related to narrative flow, is that passages from letters between the two are often not explicated in context. For illustration, Burnell, when writing of the gossip concerning Cosway and singer Luigi Marchesi (chapter 4), includes a snippet of Cosway's letter of February 6, 1789, to Jefferson. That snippet includes black "intrigues, calumnies, and injustices," but Cosway's

---

[2] John Kaminski, *Jefferson in Love: The Love Letters between Thomas Jefferson & Maria Cosway* (Lanham: Rowman & Littlefield, 2001), 38.

letter is not self-referential—she is not expressly alluding to calumnies concerning her affairs—but it is about British political corruption. Of the Jefferson-Cosway relationship, Burnell rightly acknowledges unrequited affection because of key differences in personality between the two. Jefferson is not a "forward-moving man" but an "ethereal spirit" who possesses not the will to win over the gallant, somewhat free-spirited artist.[3]

There are two other essential books that shed light on Maria Cosway.

George C. Williamson publishes *Richard Cosway, R.A.*, in 1905. The title misleads, for it is equally a biography of Maria Cosway. The book is a good starting point for scholars interested in Maria Cosway, and we are indebted to Williamson for his early research, though his critical insights are tempered by the Victorian moral strictures of his day. For instance, Williamson has access to Richard Cosway's travel diary, which crudely and bluntly tells us of his amorous affair, while married, with fellow artist Mary Moser. The diary can no longer be found, and we are wholly dependent on Williamson's account of Richard Cosway's salaciousness during his time of separation from his wife Maria, though Williamson is so disgusted by that entry that he mentions only that regard for morality demands that he overpass it without inclusion in his book and discussion of it.[4]

Gerald Barnett, in 1995, writes a biography of the Cosways and dilates considerably on the artistic side of the couple. His large contribution, following Williamson, is that he shows that both Cosways, as artists, are considerable and serious talents. Following Williamson, he, too, is a conservative critic. Barnett's reassessment does not suffer "the handicap of ridicule and malice which detractors once heaped on the name of Cosway." He adds, "Former fictions and misconceptions which distorted reality are set in focus."[5] The fictions and misconceptions to which he refers include the scandalmongery concerning the salaciousness of the Cosways, Richard especially, and critical condemnation of their abilities as artists. Barnett is inclined to take lightly all condemnations.

This book, the tripartite incentivization of which I have given above, is a collection of all the letters between Jefferson and Cosway. There is also a lengthy introduction that discusses the lives of both but focuses on Maria Cosway, for information on Jefferson's life is freely accessible. There are, in addition to the introduction, six chapters to the book. Chapters 1 through 4

---

[3] Carol Burnell, *Divided Affections: The Extraordinary Life of Maria Cosway: Celebrity Artist and Thomas Jefferson's Impossible Love* (London: Column House, 2007), 225.
[4] George C. Williamson, *Richard Cosway, R.A.* (London: George Bell and Sons, 1905).
[5] Gerald Barnett, *Richard and Maria Cosway: A Biography* (Cambridge: Lutterworht Press, 1995).

cover successively the years 1786, 1787, 1788, and 1789. Chapter 5 covers the years 1790 through 1805. As there are no known letters between 1806 and 1818, the final chapter covers the years 1819 to 1824. There are no letters exchanged in the final two years of Jefferson's life.

There are two procedural points that I make. First, all letters are from Princeton University Press' collection of Jefferson's correspondence. I include none of its copyrighted annotations and interpolations. Second, all translations from Italian to English are mine, and thus, any egregious errors in translations are mine.

I have taken certain liberties in the crafting of this book: two large and one small. First, I write beyond this preface of past events in the present tense. That I have chosen to do in some effort to bring life to them. I hope that historical purists, wedded wholly to the use of past tense to write of past events, will not find objectionable my unconventionality. Second, in translating Cosway's Italian prose into English, my aim has not been to capture her sentiments as literally as possible but to capture the meaning as precisely as possible. Thus, I sometimes add to the Italian to make plain the meaning in English. Decades of experience in translating other languages into English (e.g., Greek, Latin, German, French, and Ukrainian) has taught me well that translations, focusing too much on literalness, often obfuscate the meaning in the language to be translated. I consequently translate with a certain degree of plasticity that might irk literalists. Last, I have tended to remove all dashes in the letters where there is a change of subject, and I have separated the text, thereby making an additional paragraph. Also, I tend to break long paragraphs in letters into separate paragraphs where there is a sharp change of subject. That has the added benefit of shortening paragraphs for ease of assimilation. I justify this last liberty by appealing to Jefferson, who ever maintained the rules of a language must answer to its usage, and usage over time changes.

There are 25 figures in this book. All are public domain.

I end with a comment. This book has been a labor of love. I have thoroughly enjoyed the examination of their correspondence and critical analysis of it. It would, I maintain, make one hell of a movie!

I thank the good folks at Vernon Press for such an exemplary job of bringing the labor of love so handsomely to life!

# Introduction

## Jefferson Settles into Paris

On July 5, 1784, Thomas Jefferson, daughter Martha, and slave James Hemings board *Ceres* and sail for France. They arrive at West Cowes in 19 days and get to La Havre, France, on July 31. They arrive on August 6, and Jefferson began the taxing process of orienting himself to begin his stint, along with John Adams and Benjamin Franklin, then minister to France, as minister plenipotentiary to all nations willing to forge treaties with the fledgling United States. When Franklin retires his post as minister to France one year later, Jefferson is offered and accepts the position, which will keep him in Paris until September 1789.[1]

Why does Jefferson accept an invitation to be minister plenipotentiary?

Independent of the fact that Jefferson is abundantly qualified to be a minister plenipotentiary, there are two singular events that lead to his decision to accept the post of ambassador.

First, his two-year stint as wartime governor of Virginia—from June 1, 1779, to June 2, 1781—proves to be an overwhelming and humiliating experience. While furnishing Virginians as soldiers for the Continental Army under the command of Gen. George Washington, Jefferson does all that he can to keep Virginia safe from the encroachments of British forces during the Revolutionary War in his state. His actions on behalf of the nation and Virginia, at the end of his second year, put himself and his family at great risk, as Col. Banastre Tarleton forays into Charlottesville to capture Gov. Jefferson and other key figures and to purloin important documents. Jefferson eludes Tarleton, who does what he can to get his revenge on the small town by destroying magazines and disbursing the Virginian Assembly. When Jefferson resigns his post on completion of his second term with the expectation that another, with military experience, will succeed him, he is flabbergasted to find that a motion has passed in Virginia's House of Delegates to investigate his behavior in office for possible dereliction of duty—*viz.*, cravenness.

Second, after a long and laborious pregnancy in which daughter Lucy Elizabeth is born, wife Martha, weakened and sickly, becomes moribund. She dies on September 6 at the young age of 33. Jefferson is buried with grief.

---

[1] In the account I here give, I follow my book, *Thomas Jefferson in Paris: The Ministry of a Virginian "Looker-on"* (Wilmington, DE: Vernon Press, 2022), introduction.

Removal from Monticello for several months is a way of removing himself from France for some time for the residence he has built as a shrine to his wife.[2]

The story begins thus. After having settled himself in France later in 1784, Jefferson, ever with a strong interest in the fine arts, meets and befriends American painter John Trumbull (1756–1843) in London in April 1785. Jefferson invites the talented young artist to stay with him and soak up the artistic climate of Paris. Trumbull happily accepts Jefferson's largesse and stays with him at Hôtel de Langeac beginning in July 1786.

Trumbull is, early in life, both a scholar and soldier. He matriculates at Harvard College in 1771 and graduates two years later. He later participates in the Revolutionary War as second aide-de-camp to Gen. Washington, but resigns in 1777 over disagreement concerning the date of his commission as officer.

Shortly thereafter, Trumbull turns to painting—an odd choice of profession given that he loses almost wholly the use of one eye in an accident as a child. He removes to London in 1780 to study painting with Benjamin West, who encourages Trumbull to focus on miniature paintings, then in vogue, and small paintings of the Revolutionary War. After suffering through certain political difficulties in London, Trumbull later paints *Battle of Bunker Hill* and *Death of General Montgomery in the Attack on Quebec*.

**Figure I-1:** John Trumbull's Self-Portrait, c. 1802

Source: Yale University Art Gallery

---

[2] M. Andrew Holowchak, *Thomas Jefferson in Paris: The Ministry of a Virginian "Looker on"* (Wilmington, DE: Vernon Press, 2022), introduction.

Introduction

It was difficult for painters in Jefferson's day to survive even in the intellectual circles of large cities like Paris and London, where the fine arts flourish among the *bon ton*, without the sponsorship of some wealthy personage. Painting is a fine art—*viz.*, not something to be appreciated for the uses to which it can be put, but it is to be appreciated for itself. There are far too many painters for all, even the most capable, to find sponsorship. Moreover, many have little sense of the aesthetic. Most eke out a living through sycophancy or cleverness in portraits: e.g., crafting an inordinately flattering portrait of a subject or replication of a famous painting that captures a significant historical event and placing the face of a buyer into the painting. Furthermore, painters at the time had a questionable status. Louis-Sébastien Mercier, in his *Le Tableau de Paris*, lists them just above artisans, manual laborers, servants, and the poor, and below princes and high lords; lawyers, clergy, and medical doctors; financiers; and merchants. He writes: "Artists' lives are dissipated and sometimes immoral; that of artisans is sober; perhaps because they are dedicated to occupations that are more useful than the arts that cater to luxury, they are compensated by a clear conscience and a tranquil life. A woodworker strikes one as more trustworthy than a painter of enamels." Artists feed off the wealthy and relatively useless French nobility, he continues somewhat tongue-in-cheek, who "claim descent going back to *Adam*."[3]

The friendship between Jefferson and Trumbull is mutually beneficial. Jefferson offers much moral encouragement for Trumbull to proceed as a painter of Early American history, and Trumbull's works, in the eyes of Jefferson, will help to chronicle visually the events related to the American Revolution. During Jefferson's trip to England, Trumbull takes his host to visit his mentor, Benjamin West, as well as painters John Singleton Copley and Mather Brown, another student of West. Jefferson will pose for Brown in the now well-known painting, finished in 1786 and in the possession of John Adams and his family till 1999, when it is acquired by Monticello.[4]

Of his Jefferson's patronage, Trumbull writes in his journal:

> In the summer of 1785, political duties had called Mr. Jefferson, then minister of the United States in Paris, to London, and there I became acquainted with him. He had a taste for the fine arts, and highly approved my intention of preparing myself for the accomplishment of a

---

[3] Louis-Sébastien Mercier, *Panorama of Paris: Selections from* Le Tableau de Paris *by Louis-Sébastien Mercier*, ed. Jeremy D. Popkin (University Park: The Pennsylvania State University Press, 1999), 216–17.

[4] It is now next to Brown's painting of Adams. Of that painting, William Short said it was "an étude [as] it has no feature like him." William Short to John Trumbull, 10 Sept. 1788.

national work. He encouraged me to persevere in this pursuit, and kindly invited me to come to Paris, to see and study the fine works there, and to make his house my home, during my stay.[5]

As Trumbull's entry in his journal indicates, he is the chief beneficiary of his stay, beginning in the late summer of 1786, with Jefferson. The artist is, in effect, given his own studio at Hôtel de Langeac. It is, as William Howard Adams notes, "a casual yet significant gesture that was without precedent,"[6] just another instance of Jefferson's bigheartedness and generosity, for as perusal of Trumbull's *Autobiography* shows, the young and talented artist will struggle through much of his life to win the sort of notoriety and fame that will enable him to be financially stable and relatively self-sufficient. There is no evidence that Jefferson's "sponsorship" of Trumbull is remunerative, but the latter does have food to eat, a place to stay, and verbal encouragement while he studies his art in France, while Jefferson encourages Trumbull to "chronicle" key events of the American Revolution for posterity through his paintings.[7] Trumbull's most famous painting is perhaps the twelve-by-eighteen-foot *Declaration of Independence* (Figure I-2), which depicts the five-man committee, commissioned to draft the document—including Adams, Franklin, and Jefferson—presenting the Declaration to the Congress for its assessment on June 28, 1776.[8]

Trumbull will also paint a miniature of Jefferson in 1788—an oil on wood (4" x 3¼"), which Trumbull will leave behind for Jefferson, when Trumbull returns to England late in 1788. The miniature Trumbull creates from his depiction of Jefferson in his *Declaration*. He will make two other miniatures of Jefferson from his *Declaration*, each distinctive. Figure I-3 shows a casual Jefferson. He has a full crop of ruddy-brown hair. The shoulders are square to the canvas, while Jefferson's head is turned sharply to his left. The lips are slightly pursed and the eyes are grave. The whitish cheeks show only a touch of exposure to the sun.

---

[5] John Trumbull, Autobiography, in *Reminiscences and Letters of John Trumbull, from 1756 to 1841* (New Haven: Wiley and Putnam, 1841), 96–97.

[6] William Howard Adams, *The Paris Years of Thomas Jefferson* (New Haven: Yale University Press, 1997), 91.

[7] See also TJ to David Humphreys (14 Aug. 1786): "Your friend Mr. Trumbul [sic] was here at present. He brought his Bunker's hill and Death of Montgomery to have them engraved here. He was yesterday to see the king's collection of paintings at Versailles, and confesses it surpassed every thing of which he even had an idea. I persuaded him to stay and study here, and then proceed to Rome."

[8] For a history of the painting, see M. Andrew Holowchak, *Jefferson in Paris: The Ministry of a Virginian "Looker-on"* (Wilmington, DE: Vernon Press, 2022), chap. 14.

*Introduction* xvii

**Figure I-2**: John Trumbull, *Declaration of Independence*, 1819

Source: U.S. Capitol

**Figure I-3:** John Trumbull, *Miniature of Jefferson*, 1788

Source: Parlor, Monticello

### Jefferson Meets Maria Cosway

On Sunday, August 6, 1786, Jefferson and Trumbull are admiring the architecturally startling dome of Halle aux Blés, the new grain market of Paris. The two chance upon artists Richard and Maria Cosway, recognized by Trumbull. Jefferson is quickly under the spell of young Maria—a woman, 26 at the time and of urbanity, beauty, talent, and gentility. All in the quartet agree to spend together the remainder of the day, and that is likely on Jefferson's insistence.

There are albatrosses. Jefferson has a dinner engagement that evening with none other than the Duchess d'Enville (Marie Louise Elisabeth de la Rochefoucauld) and the Cosways have their own engagement, so those in the party send "lying messengers" to cancel those engagements. Jefferson, Trumbull, and the Cosways spend the day enjoying a variety of experiences from dinner at Café Mecanique—clearly Jefferson's idea, for he wishes to impress the Cosways with the food being served via a dumbwaiter from below—to a mix of other entertainments, including the fireworks of Ruggieri's Garden and a visit to the great composer Johann Baptist Krumpholtz to hear the music of the harp.

**Figure I-4:** Maria Cosway, *Self-Portrait*, 1778

Source: Uffizi Gallery, Florence, Italy

Maria Louisa Catherine Cecelia Hadfield (1759–1838) is born to English parents in Italy in 1759. Her father, Charles Hadfield (1725–1776), is born in Shrewsbury, England, of a wealthy merchant. He moves to Italy and starts an

*Introduction* xix

inn called Carlo's in Palazzo Medici, Italy, near Basilica di Santo Spirito. It overlooks the River Arno and caters to English travelers and specializes in British fare. Her mother, Elizabeth Pocock (1726–1782), is wed to Charles in 1753 by a certain Rev. Lepeatt and will change her name to Isabella. They will have Maria in 1760.[9]

**Figure I-5:** Thomas Patch, *Charles Hadfield*, n.d.

Source: The Collection of the late Cyril and Shirley Fry

Maria gives this account of her father's career—being an owner of an inn is not the most respectable occupation—and the meeting of her parents. "My father was a brave and honest Englishman of Manchester, came to Italy, settled in Florence, saw with pain that his compatriots were badly housed, took a fine palazzo, opened an inn with English taste, met my mother who was traveling with an English family, married her."[10] He will own three inns—each highly successful and unique in that they, upscale when compared to Italian inns, cater to the English habits and tastes of visiting British people.

One of the frequent guests at the inn is Thomas Patch (1725–1782), an eccentric English caricaturist and talented landscape painter. Cocksure, mumpish, volatile, and banished from Rome for "his oddities and loose way of talking in all companies" (*viz.*, his homosexuality), he removes to Florence

---

[9] Carol Burnell, *Divided Affections: The Extraordinary Life of Maria Cosway: Celebrity Artist and Thomas Jefferson's Impossible Love* (London: Column House, 2007), 3.
[10] Carol Burnell, *Divided Affections*, 3–4.

where he will flourish and remain till his death, begin landscapes of Florence and caricatures in the manner of P.L. Ghezzi, and become fast friends with Sir Horace Mann, whose residence, Palazzo Manetti, is very near to the inn. Three of his landscapes of Florence, which he calls "bridge-paintings," will be purchased by King George III. Patch's paintings of high society exhibit a penchant for denigration. *A Punch Party in Florence* (Figure I-6), in Carlo's Inn, offers an example through dissipation. The stage is Charles Hadfield's own Carlo's Inn. Fourteen men engage in tête-è-tête conversations while the host, Charles Hatfield, holds up a large bowl of punch. The convivialists (from left end, behind table, and to right end) are Sir H. Mainwaring, Earl Cowper, Viscount Torrington, Lord Grantham (with tray of cameos), Rev. J. Lipyeatt, Earl of Stamford (right arm extended to show a just-bought cameo), Jacob Houblon, Charles Hatfield, Earl of Moray, and Charles S. Boothby; and, from left to right and depicted in front of the table, James Whyte, Sir Brook Bridges, Sir John Rushout, and Sir Charles Bunbury.[11]

**Figure I-6:** Thomas Patch, *Punch Party in Florence,* 1760.

Source: National Trust Collections, Dunham Massey, Cheshire, England.

---

[11] F.J.B. Watson, "Thomas Patch: Notes on His Life, Together with a Catalogue of His Known Works," *The Volume of the Walpole Society,* Vol. 28, 1939–1940: 22–26.

## Introduction

The paintings on the wall are of Dionysus—god of drunkenness, merriment, orgy, and ecstasy, and pulled by leopards—and Silenus, companion, and tutor to Dionysus—god of ecstasy, drunkenness, dancing, music, and foul gestures, and pulled by tigers. The small statue is the Dancing Faun with clappers in hands, a replica of the original in the Uffizi. Its socle shows the Medici's arms. That and a fallen chair, tipped and broken bottles on the floor, and, in general, the slovenliness (e.g., the seated figure of Bunbury, third from right, with sock falling, is too inebriated for conversation) suggest the possibility of soon-to-come tohubohu, perhaps through homosexual release. A nearly invisible small brown dog in the right corner of the event stares in disbelief. The patch includes himself in the bust, top-right. He sports faun's ears and short faun's horns, symbols of merry-making, abandonment, and the wilderness. Early experiences of conviviality and boisterousness at the inn while a child certainly makes a lasting impression on Maria, who will ever have a desire for some degree of profligacy.

Young Maria Hadfield and her six siblings are under the care of an insane nurse, Brigida, who poisons four of her siblings and intends to make Maria the fifth. Says Maria, who writes decades later of the maid's intendment, in a singular autobiographical letter to future husband Richard Cosway's cousin, Sir William Cosway (24 May 1830), "I have sent four to heaven [and] I hope to send you also." Her villainy is disclosed, and the nursemaid claims that she has murdered the children to offer them straight passage to heaven in an effort to protect them from the Protestantism of her parents.[12] As sensationalist as the account seems—would not the parents have been suspicious after the death of the first two children?—there is nothing in contradiction to it, and the account, taken as given, is further evidence of the bedlam of life at the inn.

With the nurse's insanity disclosed, the distraught child is placed at the age of four to convalesce in a Catholic convent, *Il Conventino*—she will be raised as Catholic, not Protestant, to shield her from the animosity of the Catholics in Italy—where she will be nurtured and doted on there by the gentle Italian nuns, who teach her geography, history, Italian, French, embroidery, and music. She will become adept at the organ, harp, and harpsichord. By six, Maria will play the organ at the convent and begin to compose her own airs.[13]

The quiet, security, and loving attention that Maria experiences at the convent is radially unlike her life at the inn, where it is loud, the pace is fast, and she

---

[12] Gerald Barnett, "Appendix VI: Selected Letters," *Richard and Maria Cosway: A Biography* (Cambridge: The Lutterworth Press, 1995), 260. This letter, written late in life, contains some of the most singular information on Maria's past, though cautious historians will be guarded, given the discursive nature of the long letter and its remoteness from many of the events recalled.

[13] Gerald Barnett, "Appendix VI," 260.

cannot receive the affection needed by a young girl whose parents, flitting around the inn, are fixed on money-making for the financial security of their children. Her years in the convent, with some time each week to return to the boisterous inn, will make a profound impression on Maria and come to signify, even embody, throughout her life, one of two antipodal ideals: tranquil security of the ascetic life with Catholic trimmings. The other antipode, the frenzied bustle of the hedonic life, the life of sinful indulgence, is impressed on her from life at the inn. Throughout her life, she will pinball from the two extremes: asceticism after too much indulgence in hedonism and hedonism after too much exposure to asceticism. Thus, she will have lifelong penchants for profligacy and penitence. She will never find the sort of peace that Jefferson finds in authenticity.

Those contraries are manifest in two dreams young Maria has while at the convent. She wrote to her first musical tutor and famous portrait artist Violante Siries Cerrotti in 1781 of them (my italics for the dreams). I return to Cerrotti momentarily.

> I'll always remember what you now repeat to me "that the promises made on the yearning for the religious condition, if not fulfilled, may become fatal and in no other condition can one ever enjoy the happiness sought there." I always remember the explanation you gave me of the dream I had during my childhood at the convent. *I was playing in a vast hall with some of my friends when I saw the ceiling open and, out of the clouds, the Virgin appeared with the Child. They descended to earth and started to lift me up but they returned me again.*
>
> I cried so much that I awoke but I fell asleep again and *the same Virgin came and lifted me up to heaven for ever.* You told me then, "It seems to mean that half your life you will aspire to heaven, but you will come back to the world; but the second part of the dream shows great hopes of happiness; remember this." If the first dream was frightening, the second was of great comfort. I put my trust in your prayers. ... My mind still retains the strong impression you made upon my heart.[14]

The passage is singular, as it shows the profound, indelible impression of the dream on young Maria. Biographer Carol Burnell explains the dream—she takes both as one—as Maria's ceaseless and ever-present desire to retire to a convent to live out her life, ever frustrated by the exigencies of reality, e.g., the encroachments of a mother or the secretive activities of her salacious

---

[14] Gerald Barnett, "Appendix VI," 260.

*Introduction* xxiii

husband.¹⁵ As we shall see, the cloistered life is not, for Cosway, Elysium. It is significant, instead, for what it is not—the bustle and decadence of the real world—not for what it is. Thus, it functions as a retreat for Cosway and has the effect on her, as does the confessional for a Catholic. Cosway can handle the real world so long as she can occasionally escape from it—*viz.*, so long as she can occasionally "confess." Consequently, a simpler explanation for the first dream is her early exposure to and lifelong penchant for hedonism, which does not square well with ascetic Catholicism. It is Maria's way of saying to herself, *I wish certainly to be for eternity with the Madonna in Heaven, but before I settle into amaranthine quiet bliss, I first would like to live it up a bit.*

What of the second brief dream?

This succinct dream is Cosway telling herself that she, overall, will, when the time is right, be forgiven—be lifted up to heaven.

The letter to Cerrotti is ever to be weighed when considering Maria's later life. First, it illustrates, through her dreams, the need in her life for some expression of both virtue and vice. The life of virtue is tranquil and quiet but lifeless and dull; the life of vice is vivacious and exciting but loud and exhausting. Second, it exemplifies the profound and ineffable impression that Cerrotti has made on Maria from early life. Cerrotti, it seems, has had a deeper influence on Maria than Maria's mother.

When she is eight, Maria suffers a life-altering experience: observing another girl in the process of drawing. Maria thereafter takes to sketching and learns about colors. The sisters notice her uncommon talent and allow Maria to be instructed by Cerrotti (1709–1783, Figure I-7), a master of crayons and watercolors and an artist who has studied under François Boucher and Hyacinthe Rigaud in Paris for five years. The tutorial lasts for some four years and ends when Maria is 12. Cerrotti admits that she has taught Maria all that she knows, and the core of that tutorial is certainly religious instruction. Qua artist, it is time for Maria to study under another with superior instincts and skills.

At this kairotic time, German painter Johann Zoffany (1733–1810) appears in Florence. He has been commissioned to paint *La Tribuna* (Figure I-8)—an octagonal room of the famous gallery of the Grand Duke of Medici that houses some of the world's greatest artist treasures of the day, including the sculptures/busts *Dancing Faun* (Ancient Roman), *Venus de Medicio* (Cleomenes), *Zeus-Serapis* (Ancient Roman), and *The Two Wrestlers* (Ancient Roman) as well as the paintings *Portrait of Galileo Galilei* (Justus Sustermans),

---

¹⁵ Carol Burnell, *Divided Affections*, 11.

*Portrait of Perugino* (Raphael), *The Four Philosophers* (Rubens), and *Madonna* (Guido Reni).

**Figure I-7:** Violante Cerrotti, *Self-Portrait*, n.d.

Source: AWA Archives, Florence, Italy

Zoffany takes certain liberties with the depiction. His aim is not to include all the works that are in the room at the time, but only the most significant, and he brings into the room artworks from other rooms in the gallery and rearranges the works for the best effect. He paints himself (fourth from left, standing, and holding up a painting) and other dignitaries (e.g., Sir John Dick, John Gordon, Thomas Patch, and Sir Horace Mann) into the painting. Charles Hadfield, at some point, makes the acquaintance of the famous painter and arranges for the painter to school his talented daughter.[16] Through Zoffany, Maria will have access to La Tribuna to study the multifarious techniques of those masters featured there. There is no question of her acquaintance with Zoffany being a life-altering experience. In addition to sketches, paintings, and sculptures, Maria will see, among the collectibles of the duke, waxen figures, stuffed animals, animals' horns, exotic furniture, and numerous books with depictions of artworks.

---

[16] Carol Burnell, *Divided Affections*, 12.

*Introduction*

**Figure I-8:** Johann Zoffany, *La Tribuna*, 1772–1778.

Source: Royal Collection, Windsor

During her time at the Duke's gallery, Maria will meet world-class artists such as Anton Raphael Mengs.[17] While under the tutelage of Zoffany, whose tutorial is a matter of having Maria copy certain of the best portraits of the gallery, she will decide to make painting the focus of her life.

Maria falls under the spell of painter Sir Joshua Reynolds (1723–1792) when his self-portrait is brought to and hanged in the gallery. "The colouring is so beautiful that it throws to the ground all the other portraits, especially that of Sir Mengs (Rafael), which is just above it."[18] Reynolds pushes Maria beyond what she takes as the relative lifelessness of Mengs' Neo-Classicism.

Maria soon meets Joseph Wright, whose influence is that of advice, in the summer of 1775. Wright shares his opinion that she will never become illustrious by always copying the portraits of great masters. The implication is that studying under Zoffany, while it opens Maria to the world of great painters, will benefit her

---

[17] Carol Burnell, *Divided Affections*, 13.
[18] Carol Burnell, *Divided Affections*, 16.

only so much.[19] Later that summer, Maria will make the acquaintance of young male English artists—Henry Tresham, Edward Edwardes, and Ozias Humphry—who have come to Florence to study and practice. When the young men leave after the summer and retreat to Rome, Maria falls into a routine, which she describes in a letter to Humphry: copying pictures from 9 a.m. till 1 p.m., study of architecture after lunch till 4:30 p.m., singing at 5 p.m., drawing from 6 to 9 p.m., and the opera in the evening. She writes of making a sacrifice to Apollo and Daphne during the night "because, for me, it is a sacrifice to have to stay and watch such ugly dancing."[20]

**Figure I-9:** Joshua Reynold, *Self-Portrait*, 1775

Source: Uffizi Gallery, Florence, Italy.

The routine, at first blush, seems irremediably dull in its redundancy. Yet Maria's parting comment about the ugly dancing shows that she is becoming a critic of the fine arts through exposure to the rigor and hedonic release of the artistic manner of life. That comes out in letters in the winter from late 1775 to early 1776. Writes Carol Burnell:

---

[19] The apprenticeship was likely a matter of a smattering of comments by the master, when he pulled himself away from his own work.
[20] Carol Burnell, *Divided Affections*, 19.

Maria's letters during the winter of 1776–1776 reveal a young girl discovering the world and its pleasures with delight. She adores music, the opera, painting, dancing, and sharing her passions with her friends, ... all young men. She does not mention other young girls nor does she seem bent on a religious vocation as she professed later in life. For a girl of fifteen she already displays critical judgment in her appreciation of different musical artists and painters, comparing [sic] the castrato Rubinelli with Milico or judgeing Sir Joshua Reynolds far superior to Mengs.[21]

Maria is certainly aware that she is a budding, toothsome young woman in a discipline dominated by males, and that makes her very appealing to many of her young male colleagues if only because she is, in a manner of speaking, the only thing of her kind on the menu. Many of her male colleagues, of course, feel shock and dismay, for there is no place for a female to study painting. She is also slowly integrating into the culture of the British *bon ton* in Florence. What limits that integration is the lack of good birth—pedigree. She has come from relative wealth but not from good blood, and that hampers Maria's movement among the society of young artists. That is clear in a passing comment by collector of art Charles Townley: "Oh, I wish she had good fortune. I would marry her directly."[22] Most artists, through success at their craft, hope to marry up, so to speak; it helps nowise to marry down.

Nonetheless, Maria is privy to nearly all social events involving the English, and there are few that she fails to attend. Social frivolity, she often admits, is an obstruction to her development as a painter. In one letter to Ozias Humphry, she admits to placing her artistry on hold because of the Carnival prior to Lent. "It has stopped me from working, I am ashamed to say; engaging in such silly amusements. ... I can see that time has passed in front of my very eyes at a fast pace and that the figure of VIRTUE is reprimanding me."[23]

In 1776, Maria avails herself of the opportunity to travel to Rome with Mr. and Mrs. Charles Gore and study the art and architecture of that grand city, where she likely visits the fantastic galleries of the villas of Cardinal Alessandro Albani and Prince Borghese. There, in November 1776—the exact day is unknown—she receives the news of the passing of her father, who has in his will left all to Maria's siblings with the exception of Maria 100 scudi.[24] Charles explains in his will (11 Apr. 1774) that Maria has had advantages throughout her life that the other children—George, William, Charlotte, and Elisabetts—did not have and

---

[21] Carol Burnell, *Divided Affections*, 20.
[22] Carol Burnell, *Divided Affections*, 17.
[23] Carol Burnell, *Divided Affections*, 24.
[24] A scudo was a large coin in circulation in Italy till the middle of the nineteenth century.

that those advantages, along with her talents in the fine arts will enable her to sift through the nodi she will encounter throughout her life.²⁵

Did Maria feel slighted by her father's will, or did she, on reflection on her father's judgment, come to agree with him? We do not know. We do know that she merely remained in Rome to complete her studies. Her friend Humphry returns to Rome and holds frequent meetings of young artists in his apartments, where Maria consorts with Henry Tresham, Henry Fuseli, and Thomas Banks.

In March 1777, Maria's mother, Isabella, tells her that William Parsons has asked for Maria's hand in marriage. Maria eventually declines the offer and instead spends much of that summer with Prince Hoare, to whom she has taken a fancy. She is of an age and of such a disposition that she will begin to turn the heads of many artists whom she meets, and she does receive several proposals of marriage but accepts none. The "advice" of her mother certainly is much in play in Maria's decisions.

Not all are moved by her comeliness and talent. James Northcote, a friend of Hoare, will later write of Maria:

> She was just eighteen years of age, not unhandsome, endowed with considerable talents, and with a form extremely delicate and a leasing manner of the utmost simplicity. But she was withal, active, ambitious, proud, and restless: she had been the object of adoration of an indulgent father, who unfortunately for her had never checked the growth of her imperfections; she had some small knowledge of painting, the same of music, and about the same of five or six languages, but was very imperfect in all these.²⁶

That assessment, however, might be due to unrequited affection, for Northcote does not mention a small knowledge of music when he first meets Maria on Christmas Eve 1778: "We now have in Rome a Miss Hadfield, who studies painting. She plays very finely on the harpsichord, and sings and composes music very finely and will be another Angelica [Kauffman]."²⁷

Maria will press on with her sketching and painting, and on September 27, 1778, she will be afforded a singular honor: She will be elected to *Accademia di*

---

²⁵ Carol Burnell, *Divided Affections*, 32.
²⁶ Stephen Lucius Gwynn, ed., *Memorials of an Eighteenth-Century Painter James Northcote* (London: T.F. Unwin, 1898), 149.
²⁷ William T. Whitley, *Artists and Their Friends in England, 1770–1799, Vol.* 2 (London: Medici Society, 1928), 149.

*Introduction* xxix

*Disegno of Florence*—the oldest academy of artists in the world. Maria is just 18 at the time of the signal honor.[28]

At some point, Isabella Hadfield, who has been doing her best to keep both open and running smoothly the inns of her husband, decides to remove her children to London. The inn's upkeeping proves to be too much without the willing help of her two sons. William wishes not to be an innkeeper, and Isabella wants the youngest son, George, to be an architect.[29] In London, too, she figures, Maria will have a greater range of well-to-do suitors from which to cull. On June 25, 1779, Isabella thus takes her family to London.

Prior to the removal, a pouty Maria slips away to Il Conventino to ask its Mother Superior if she can stay and ready herself for the cloistered life. Maria writes in her diary, "This same day I left Florence for London in the year 1781 [*sic*] against my will and they were obliged to take me out of a convent where I had decided to stay."[30] She is to be retrieved by her mother. Maria, 18, is not of age to choose for herself the life of a nun. Burnell notes that the poutiness is due to her unreturned affection for Giovanni Bastianelli—a handsome, dark-complexioned man with jet-black hair, a keen wit, and a mercurial temperament.[31] We begin to see a pattern in Maria's life. When things in the real world do not abide by her wishes, she retreats to a convent—the fount of tranquility in her early years.

Bastianelli himself proffers an account inconsistent with Maria's story of retreat to her cloister. He tells of the reception of news that "made me laugh a lot" in a letter to Prince Hoare. He writes, "Signora Maria entered the convent because of falling in love with a Florentine … and he being so indifferent and not returning this feeling, … she, out of rage at not being able to explain herself, made up all that beautiful monastic silliness. … Oh, what a lovely thing!"[32] Bastianelli's account is suggestive of Maria falling for another Florentine, not Bastianelli, though consistent with Bastianelli being that Florentine.

The picture we begin to get is of Maria as dispositionally sulky. Fine-looking but not in possession of overwhelming beauty, she attracts the attention of several suitors, but she seems incapable of winning the affection of them whom she most fancies. Bastianelli, who has visited Maria on many occasions prior to her removal to London, so enjoys Maria's distress and intimates that his visits

---

[28] Carol Burnell, *Divided Affections*, 41.

[29] Carol Burnell, *Divided Affections*, 45.

[30] Maria may have left earlier. Welch painter Thomas Jones writes that Maria left for London on May 18. *Memoirs of Thomas Jones, The Walpole Society*, Vol. 32 (O. Burridge, 1951).

[31] Carol Burnell, *Divided Affections*, 42 and 52.

[32] Carol Burnell, *Divided Affections*, 52.

to see Maria might be a sort of game to him. He aims completely to win over the brooding young lady, gain inescapable proof of her affection for him, and then crush her with ponderous indifference.

Is Bastianelli such a libertine and rogue that he finds delight in the suffering of another—in schadenfreude?

That is possible but improbable. It confirms Northcote's judgment that Maria exhibits a higher opinion of her looks and talents than she deserves, and, communicating that to others, she thereby turns off as many potential suitors as she turns on.

Bastianelli's account is also corroborative of the depiction we consistently get of Maria in her letters—and we shall see ample evidence of that in her letters to Jefferson—of an incurable manic-depressive. Abandonment to the pleasures of European society signals the manic, or hedonic, Maria; retreat to the convent, or retreat of any sort from society, like acceptance of a purely domestic role, signals religious asceticism and compunction. Maria will never be living at one of those extremes. She will never find comfort in conciliation between them. She, unlike Jefferson, is not of conciliatory matter. While Jefferson, finding agreement between his wants and thoughts and his action, is authentic; Maria, never finding agreement between her wants and thoughts and her actions, is ever inauthentic.

### The Hadfields Move to London

In London, Isabella Hadfield and her family move provisionally into 4 Berkeley Square but quickly relocate to an apartment at 8 Great George Street in Hanover Square. Once settled, they begin visits to several significant personages of London. One especially significant person is Lady Penelope Rivers, wife of the deceased Lord Rivers, George Pitt, envoy to Italy from England. Lady Rivers has readied letters of introduction to artists Sir Joshua Reynolds, whose self-portrait has overwhelmed Maria and who is then president of the Royal Academy, and the celebrated female painter Angelica Kauffman. Maria writes long after the fact to Sir William Cosway, "I had letters from Lady Rivers for all the first people of fashion. Sir J. Reynolds, Bartolozzi, Angelica Kowffman [*sic*]."[33]

Maria visits Reynolds in his studio behind his apartment. The busy painter examines some of her work and offers some light praise, but that is the extent of his "tutorial."[34]

---

[33] Gerald Barnett, "Appendix VI," 260,
[34] Carol Burnell, *Divided Affections*, 62.

*Introduction* xxxi

Maria visits the Swiss painter Angelika Kauffman, who has the distinction at the time of being the most celebrated female painter in Europe. Maria Anna Angelika Kauffmann (1741–1807, Figure I-10) has earned her reputation, in part, by eschewing portraiture in preference to historical painting, which requires not only knowledge of form and figure, but also of the Bible, history, mythology, and literature. Historical painting is, at the time, something that Maria, obviously taken by the comely and talented Kauffman, probably wishes to study under Kauffman. Yet Kauffman soon marries Antonio Zucchi and moves to Rome, and that leaves Maria to her own wiles.[35]

Maria does not and never will take to London. It is, to her, a dreary, wet, and gloomy city with a seemingly perpetual mist, exacerbated by the smog of burning coal and brick kilns. Letters are suffused with comments on the dreariness of London. On October 30, 1786, for instance, she writes to Jefferson of London's amaranthine "fog and smoke," and consequently, the "sadness … in every heart." It lacks the romance and intimacy of Florence.

**Figure I-10:** Maria Kauffmann, *Self-Portrait*, c. 1773

Source: National Portrait Gallery, London

---

[35] Carol Burnell, *Divided Affections*, 63.

The prospects of making a living in London as a painter are limited, and even accomplished artists like Humphry and Northcote fail in the city and they leave it. Artists cannot survive without patronage and they are then beholden to please their patrons—that is, compromise their art—or run the risk of losing that patronage. Maria clearly wishes to be known, like Kauffmann, as a prominent historical painter, not a portraitist. So, Maria's prospects of making a living by praxis of her art are poor. It helps nowise that she is not of good blood and that she is Catholic.

Through acquaintance with Charles Townley, a collector of art whom the Marias meets in Florence and has since moved to London where he completes a large townhouse for his collection, Maria meets Richard Cosway.[36]

Richard Cosway (1742–1821) is 17 years older, shorter than her, and a definite mismatch apropos of physical attractiveness and spirituel. Though short, thin, and unattractive, Richard Cosway "compensates" through vibrancy and *savoir faire*. Moreover, he is a fop—what the British call "macaroni," that is, someone who lives in England but dresses foppishly, as if he were in Italy or France. In that, he is not alone, but he is part of the Macaroni Brotherhood.[37] Macaroni is likely an image that Richard intentionally constructs to segregate himself from the many other aspiring British artists to advance his career. It is also likely a way of disguising his physical defects: shortness and unattractiveness. Cosway, who will be called "monkey"[38] on account of his smallness and smarminess, will, however, become a brilliant, innovative, and successful painter of portraits, miniatures especially, and he is one of the key figures that makes wanted miniatures, which are not especially prized at the time because they are not especially done well. That Richard Cosway focuses on portraiture, not historical paintings, says much about his aspirations. Interest in prestige and money overrides interest in being recognized as a world-class painter, though Williamson notes that Cosway aims as a youth "to be some day the greatest artist in London."[39]

Yet Cosway's success in portraiture is much due to his talent as a painter. He experiments with innovations in painting miniatures with enamels. Writes Gerald Barnett:

---

[36] Gerald Barnett, *Richard and Maria Cosway*, 51.
[37] Gerald Barnett, *Richard and Maria Cosway*, 32. Consider the song "Yankee Doodle": "Yankee Doodle went to town / A-riding on a pony / He stuck a feather in his hat / And called it macaroni."
[38] Says John Thomas Smith, "Cosway though a well-made little man, was certainly very much like a monkey in his face." *John Thomas Smith, Nollekens and His Times*, Vol. II (London, 1829), 407.
[39] George Charles Williamson, *Richard Cosway, R.A.* (London: George Bell and Sons, 1905), 6.

Cosway's miniature technique, brought about by constant practice and devotion to improvement, was showing noticeable change and advance by the early 1780s. He experimented so as to enhance the translucent effect of pigments on an ivory base, and this led him to produce portraits of increased size. The traditional eighteenth[-]century miniature had usually been between one and two inches in height. By custom, a good deal of gum had been added to the pigments, which minimized the transparent quality of ivory when this was increasingly used as a base. With an emphasis on plain backgrounds and the frequent employment of body color, this had tended to place unnecessary handicaps on the miniature as an art form.[40]

**Figure I-11:** Richard Cosway, Self-portrait in charcoal with water coloring, n.d.

Source: Uffizi Gallery, Florence, Italy

Richard Cosway's self-portrait in charcoal with water coloring (Figure I-11) typifies his talent for flattery: here, self-flattery. Cosway appears as a conquering and handsome Roman emperor, as he stands stout, stately, earthfast, and erudite. A stout left leg fixes him to the floor (suggestive of

---

[40] Gerald Barnett, *Richard and Maria Cosway*, 63.

firmness), the right leg is relaxed atop a solid sphere (suggestive of dominion over the earth), and his arms seem easily to hold a massive tome (suggestive of strength and erudition). There is nothing of the monkey or macaroni in this portrait. Cosway will often create highly flattering self-portraits, symptomatic both of self-conceit as well as insecurity, though it is to be conceded that many other artists of the time do the same. Artistry is a highly competitive career, and talent without self-conceit is perhaps insufficient for success. Cosway's self-portraits that include his future wife, Maria, show her submissiveness to him, a manly, not monkeyish, man deserving of condescension in his presence.

Despite Cosway's spirituel and comportment, he is, unbeknown to Maria, a libertine, and he travels with Townley in libertine circles. Evidence of Cosway's crassness and ribaldry is evident in a letter to Charles Townley.

> There can be no <u>Life</u> here without you, Wynne is quite envellop'd in cunt—but, alas, tis his Wife's—I believe you don't envy him. ... With respect to shagging A is much the same as when you left us (your part omitted,)—but as to myself I stick as close to Radicati's arse as a Bum Bailif to Lord Deloraine's—Italy for ever say I—if the Italian women fuck as well in Italy as they do here, you must be happy indeed—I am such a zealot for them that I'd be damned if ever I fuck an English woman again (if I can help it) by the time you return I will almost venture to pronounce you may fuck the first Woman you meet? Let her be who she will—as there are no less than eight divorces on the tapis in Doctors Commons since you departed—a <u>clergyman</u> has just published openly a treatise on fucking under the title of the Joys of Hymen—so that upon the whole you see things go on as they shou'd do—... Adio—nothing on earth (fucking Radicati always excepted) can make me so happy as hearing from you, when you have house relaxation from virtue[41] & fucking.[42]

The letter, crass, shows a mind preoccupied with the carnality that only lush living can reward. While Cosway certainly enjoys his craft as a fine art—that is, an art that is to be enjoyed in itself—he certainly also knows that a talented artist can expect to enjoy many licentious perks.

Richard Cosway gains fame with his first miniature of George, the Prince of Wales (1762–1830, Figure I-12), in 1780. George is a young dandy, meticulously attired and effeminate in appearance. Cosway quickly wins the approbation of the prince and soon becomes "First Painter to the Most Serene Prince of Wales" ("*Primarius Pictor Serenissimi Walliae Principis*"), who will, in time, become

---

[41] Expertise in the fine arts, and not to be conflated with "virtue."
[42] Carol Burnell, *Divided Affections*, 422.

*Introduction* xxxv

King George IV. The prince is also known to be a libertine, and Cosway thereafter will pander to George's dissipation in a number of ways, e.g., by painting erotic scenes on George's snuff boxes and perhaps even offering his future wife for the enjoyment of the prince.[43] As the prince's official painter, Richard is responsible for painting George's various mistresses, overseeing and adding to his collection of artworks, decorating the prince's Carleton House, and being nearby when George wants him to be nearby, perhaps often as his lover.[44]

**Figure I-12:** Richard Cosway, *George, the Prince of Wales*, c. 1781

Source: National Portrait Gallery, London

Having met Maria at Townley's place, Cosway calls on her at her residence on St. George Street and makes some impression—at least on Maria's mother. Cosway will soon speak to Isabella Hadfield about Maria's hand in marriage. Isabella will speak to Maria, who initially is revolted by the notion, but Isabella ultimately convinces her daughter that her fate and her younger siblings' fate depends on Maria accepting the proposal. Having sold their inns and taken

---

[43] There is ready access to the prince's Carlton House, as the garden of Schombery House had a private pathway to Carlton House.
[44] William Howard Adams, *The Paris Years of Thomas Jefferson* (New London: Yale University Press, 1997), 101–4.

with them all that they have to London, the Hadfields are nearing financial ruin. Artist James Northcote sums up Maria's circumstances in his diary.

> She came over to England after the death of her father in company with her mother, two brothers, and two sisters, filled with the highest expectations of being the wonder of the nation like another Angelica Kauffman. But alas! These expectations failed; the money which the father had gained in Florence was quickly spent in England, and the family were [sic] soon in some degree of distress. This change, to her so very great, she bore with admirable fortitude and magnanimity, but in the end, after having refused better offers in her better days, she from necessity married Cosway, the miniature painter,[45] who at that time adored her, though she always despised him.[46]

The two will wed on January 18, 1781, at St. George's Church of Hanover Square—Maria is 20 at the time—and Cosway will slowly indoctrinate his wife, whose English is poor, into high British society. Maria, in a late-in-life autobiographical letter to Sir William Cosway, sums up her situation: "I became acquainted with Mr. Cosway[,] his offer was accepted, my Mother[']s wishes gratified & I married tho' under age. –I kept very retired for a twelve-month until I became acquainted with the society I should form, the effect of the exhibition, the taste & character of the Nation."[47] Shielding Maria from the British *bon ton* is necessary, at least until she gains acquaintancy with British customs and better facility with proper, non-vulgar English. Maria's sentiments, it is important to note, say nothing about *her* willingness to enter the relationship. Yet once she is adequately indoctrinated in the society of England's *bon ton*, she will enjoy the company of its largest people and those expected to be the new large.

We can reasonably assume that Maria becomes relatively fast acquainted with Richard's world of perversity—it is inconceivable that he could hide that from her—yet we have no direct evidence of her finding that insufferable.

Carol Burnell presumes that their relationship is easy and even sometimes happy. Though he has not married a woman with a dowry, Richard is mindful that he has, in the physical sense, married much above his expectations in a manner that can only advance his situation, and he is, at least early on, probably at least privately obsequious and willing to cater to every whim of Maria. His cheeriness, good humor, love of scuttlebutt, and penchant for hyperbole Maria finds pleasant. Moreover, she will literally come to swim in

---

[45] An obvious slap at Cosway for being merely a painter of portraits.
[46] Carol Burnell, *Divided Affections*, 71.
[47] Gerald Barnett, "Appendix VI," 260.

treasures of art, books, furniture, marble, terra cottas, tapestries, Persian rugs, and other curios. There is, thus, no reason to presume, à la Northcote, that she, once married, is miserable.[48] That, of course, does not imply that she is happy. It is a marriage of convenience for both: Richard gains a toothsome wife who is a highly talented artist; Maria gains a husband with access both to the highest stratum of London's upper society and substantial money for the security of her mother and siblings.

Despite Maria's initial reluctance to have a relationship with Richard Cosway, there is unquestionably also another perk: an aesthetic upside to the relationship. Maria, through Richard, will have access to all the finest art and artists in England and access to many of Europe's finest artists when visiting Italy and France. Richard is a member of the Royal Academy, established by King George III to advance painting, sculpture, and architecture.

While married, Maria finds solace in painting and sketching, and one can readily take her choice of subjects as a portal into her inner turmoil. Her 1782 painting, *Georgiana Cavendish, Duchess of Devonshire* (Fig. I-13), is perhaps her most acclaimed painting. The duchess, 25 at the time, has become a friend of Maria. In the painting, the duchess is a celestial figure. Cosway draws inspiration for the painting from Edmund Spenser's *Faerie Queene* (1590s), where Cynthia, Goddess of the Moon, appears from the firmament. Georgiana, in Cosway's work, majestically appears from the clouds—she pushes apart them—and her appearance is triumphal. The right arm extends to the pristine celestial region, and the left arm and left leg to the begrimed earth. Her head seems to be crowned by a halo of light that sits behind it. Georgiana's gown, in places, is itself nebulous since it seems to blend into the clouds. The colors—shades of white, gray, dirty green, blue, black, and flesh—are both celestial and earthy. The browns, from a soft peanut to a dark mocha, appear on the underside of the clouds. It is impossible here not to hearken back to Maria's dream of the Madonna coming to take her to Heaven, but soon suffering a change of mind. There is in this triumphant picture the same indecision—the fight between a heavenly and earthly existence. Yet the majesty of the picture is such that one can do no other than surrender to the verdict of the goddess. Is this, in Maria's eyes, in some sense a self-portrait?

The painting is well received. One reviewer writes: "The sprightly *air* which distinguishes that *Beauty* is admirably hit off in the advancing step of the *Regent* of the night. The different shades of *azure* diffused through the piece is an argument of consistency much in favour of the artist."[49] Of that work and other

---

[48] Carol Burnell, *Divided Affections*, 76.
[49] Carol Burnell, *Divided Affections*, 94.

early works, Maria later writes: "The first pictures I exhibited made my reputation. The novelty & my Age Contributed more than the real Merit—The portrait of the Duchess of Devonshire than the Reigning beauty & fashion—in the Caracter [sic] of Cynthia from Spencer [sic] seemed to strike & other historical subjects from Shakespeare, Virgin & Homer—encouraged but never proud I followed entirely the impulse of my imagination."[50] Another critic boldly asserted that Maria Cosway is "the first of female painters" and inferior among men only to "her husband and Reynolds."[51]

**Figure I-13:** Maria Cosway, *Georgiana Cavendish*, 1782

Source: National Portrait Gallery, London

---

[50] Gerald Burnett, "Appendix VI," 260–1.
[51] Carol Burnell, *Divided Affections*, 95.

*Introduction*

Some 30 of Maria Cosway's paintings will be on exhibit in the early 1781 to 1801 at the Royal Academy: *Rinaldo, Creusa Appearing to Aeneas* (Fig. I-14), and *Like Patience on a Monument Smiling at Grief* in 1781, and in 1782, her powerful *Aeolus Raising a Storm*, which is poorly received perhaps because it is a picture of large masculinity and violence, and thus, a subject inapposite for a female, especially one who is known to be so delicate. Like her portrait of Duchess of Devonshire, there are often celestial elements in her pictures (e.g., *Georgiana Cavendish* and *Persian Woman Worshipping Rising Sun*) and the "dichotomy" of real life versus afterlife (e.g., *Creusa, Clytie* and *Aeolus*).

**Figure I-14:** Maria Cosway, *Creusa Appearing to Aeneas*, 1781

Source: Gerald Barnet. *Richard and Maria Cosway: A Biography*. (Cambridge: Lutterworth Press, 1995)

Reviews of Cosway's works will be a mixed bag. Critic Peter Pindar, who is ever at pains to say anything positive concerning the Cosways, writes derisively of Maria's depictions:

> Maria Cosway, from old Ossian's tone,
> Will bring a tale of Rawhear—so trendous!
> So full of beef, and blood, and guts, and gore.
> So stuff'd with storms and tempests—heav'n defend us!

That honest folds will shudder in their beds.
Is this too little for her: She'll do more,
And ghosts with monstrous arms, and men with monstrous heads!⁵²

Another critic writes glowingly. "This young artist (yet very young) promises to be one of the luminaries of the approaching age. Her figure, delicate and feminine to a great degree, is accompanied by a mind that emulates the boldest subjects, the grand and the terrible." The critic will go on to remark on Maria's immense talent for music. "*Cosway* is perhaps the only lady, not only in England but in Europe, who possesses an excellence so superior in the two sciences of music and painting."⁵³ Maria will exhibit four paintings at the Academy in 1783 and 1784. Reviews will be mixed, and that is perhaps not such a bad thing, given the difficulties a talented artist, let alone a talented female, encountered *en route* to success.

Figures I-13 and I-14 neatly exemplify Maria's penchant for flow and dynamism, perhaps exaggerated and theatrical, that is missing from husband Richard's works. She makes abundant use of William Hogarth's serpentine lines. Writes Hogarth in his 1770 work *The Analysis of Beauty*, "There is scarce an Egyptian, Greek, or Roman deity, but hath a twisted serpent, twisted cornucopia, or some symbol winding in this manner to accompany it."⁵⁴ For Hogarth, the serpentine line captures the essence of beauty.⁵⁵

Doubtless, on account of Richard's prurient reputation, militated for by his friendship with Prince George, and of course certainly on account of jealousy, the Cosways are subjects of much caricaturists' humor throughout the years. In 1786, engraver Francesco Bartolozzi, for instance, in Figure I-15 (1786, British Museum Satires, Catalogue of Political and Personal Satires in the Department of Prints, London), depicts a deranged "Maria Costive" (mentally slow or constipated, likely both).

---

⁵² Peter Pindar, "Ode VIII," *More Lyric Odes to the Royal Academicians* (London, 1785).
⁵³ V&A Press Cuttings, Vol. I, 194. Carol Burnell, *Divided Affections*, 98–99.
⁵⁴ William Hogarth, *The Analysis of Beauty: Written with a View of Fixing the Fluctuating Ideas of Taste* (London: J. Reeves, 1753), xviii.
⁵⁵ Hogarth was also committed to use of pyramids in pictures. That Richard Cosway followed Hogarth's strictures is plain from a small memorandum on shadows. "Figures ought always to be made Pyramidal or Serpentine and must be placed by the numbers one, two and three, this form is nowhere better seen than in ****. The figure to be painted must have its base or broady part *upwards* and its cone *downwards*." George Charles Williamson, *Richard Cosway, R.A.* (London: George Bell and Sons, 1905), 106.

Introduction    xli

**Figure I-15:** Francesco Barolozzi, *Maria Costive*, 1786

Source: "British Museum Satires". Catalogue of Political and Personal Sat-ires in the Department of Prints, London.

Though initially living at 4 Berkeley Street in Piccadilly, the Cosways in 1784 will have a large, elegant residence at Schomberg House in Pall Mall (Figure I-16). Being at this time First Painter to the Most Serene Prince of Wales, Richard Cosway's reputation is cemented, and it must be assumed that he, given his own penchant for dissolution, relishes the dissipation of the prince, and many of the prince's affairs are captured artistically by Cosway, who paints his many mistresses to the delight of the prince—what a vulgar man today might call another notch in his wooden bedpost.

The Cosways' new residence will in time, be fraught with numerous artworks of the first rank and there, they will entertain the highest and most promising of London's high society. There, the two will invite and entertain prominent and wealthy Londoners, who will play games, enjoy cards, drink tea, dine, or pose for Richard's brushstrokes. Maria will flirt with any interested men in attendance by playing her harp or harpsichord and by singing, and many of the songs are of her composition. Many men will be ensorcelled by Maria—it is easy to fall for a toothsome woman of abundant talents in the fine arts—and then Richard might arrange for them to have their portrait painted by him so that the bewitched "suitors" can again catch a glimpse, or more, of Maria while they sit.[56]

**Figure I-16:** Shomberg House. c. 1850

Source: Wikipedia

Charming so many men at their residence with her looks, *savoir faire*, and musical talent—Maria is, as hostess of Schomberg House, a professional enchantress—it is easy to see why Jefferson will become devotedly smitten with her.

---

[56] John Kaminski, "A Delicious Romance: The Charming American Diplomat and the Exquisite European Artist," *The Journal of Thomas Jefferson's Life and Times*, Vol. 1, Ed. 1, 2018, 45–57.

Chapter I

# The Year 1786

Richard Cosway, in 1786, is invited to Paris by Louise Philippe II, Duc d'Orléans (1747–1793), cousin of King Louis XVI of France, who wishes Cosway to paint his family at his residence in the magnificent Palais-Royal.[1] The duke, a libertine, has had numerous affairs with women of his day and many bastard children. In spite of his sexual libertinage, he will marry Louise Marie Adélaïde de Bourbon, who brings a large dowry and much land to the marriage and will have by her six children. And so, the invitation to Richard Cosway to come to Paris is no accident. The duke certainly has heard of Cosway's salaciousness as well as his talent as an artist, and Philippe, wishing to have portraits done of his family, aims to have a person, qua artist, simpatico. For Maria, it will be an opportunity to leave the amaranthine dreariness of London for a more congenial climate. On July 16, the two depart for Paris.

The Cosways will lodge on Rue Coq-Héron and likely at Hôtel Parlement d'Anglettere, located in Central Paris and to the north of River Seine. Prior to readiness for the duke, the Cosways take in all the famous galleries in London and become acquainted with the *haut monde* of Paris. They too shortly become reacquainted with American painter John Trumbull, whom they have met in London and who is staying with American ambassador Thomas Jefferson, whom we have already seen will meet the Cosways with Trumbull on August 6.

What is Jefferson's initial impression of Maria Cosway?

As we shall see from Jefferson's protracted Head-and-Heart letter to Maria on October 16, written shortly after her departure from Paris to London, it is reasonably clear that Jefferson is immediately taken by Cosway.

What is Maria's initial impression of Thomas Jefferson?

That is difficult to ascertain. Cosway certainly notes that he—tall, lightly complected, gangly, and unassuming in presence both by his thinness and demeanor—is somewhat of a physical oddity. He is not unattractive. She certainly notes that he is a man who is very knowledgeable apropos of the fine arts, especially architecture, though he is no artist. She probably does not come to know the breadth of Jefferson's knowledge, which she will later come to

---

[1] The Cosways have visited France the year prior in large part for Maria's convalenscence and plan on a return in 1786.

know, as Jefferson is ever sufficiently accommodating and polite to converse with people pursuant to their own interests, not to converse on subjects to the disadvantage of his interlocutors. She certainly notes that Jefferson, unlike her macaroni husband, is authentic—*viz.*, that Jefferson is not concerned with being French-like in France or British-like in Britain, but merely with being the person that he is. He is certainly a man remarkably different from her husband, who is a bit of a chameleon.

It is likely that Cosway is intrigued by Jefferson, but unlikely that she feels any sort of immediate attraction to him. From her experiences with other men, she probably is of disposition to see if someone is smitten with her before showing any interest in him. There have been too many for whom she has felt affection and who have not felt similarly.

Jefferson and Maria Cosway, sometimes alone and sometimes with the company of husband Richard or with an escort like Trumbull, thereafter will spend together their Parisian days during the remainder of the summer as two lovers of the fine arts—visiting artists, attending concerts, examining the architecture of churches and public buildings, dining with aristocrats, studying the various formal French gardens (*Jardin du Roi*, especially), and visiting shops, inasmuch as the opportunities avail themselves. They will visit Comte d'Orsay, whose house is filled with fine paintings, bronze pieces, and porcelain; painters Elisabeth Vigée-Lebrun, Jacques-Louis David, and Hubert Robert; Comte de Moustier and Comte de Vaudreuil; Abbé Calut and Abbé Arnoux; and Madame de Bréhan and Madame de Staël, among other famous Parisian ladies.

From this late summer of their acquaintance and to the end of the year, Jefferson and Maria will exchange 12 letters—six by Jefferson and six by Cosway. As the letters of this year and other years show, it is clear that Maria does not think of Jefferson as just another "suitor." Her letters—both their number and tone—show genuine affection for Jefferson, though they offer no evidence of the deep affection Jefferson expresses in certain letters to her.

## "I meant to have had the pleasure of seeing you twice"

## MC to TJ, Paris, 20 Sept. 1786

[I hope] you dont always judge by appearances [otherwise it wo]uld be Much to My disadvantage this day, without [me] deserving it; it has been the day of contradiction, I meant to have had the pleasure of seing you Twice, and I have appeard a Monster for not having sent to know how you was, the whole day. I have been More uneasy, Than I can express. This Morning My Husband kill'd My project, I had proposed to him, by burying himself among Pictures and forgeting the hours, though we were Near your House coming to see you, we were obliged to turn back, the time being much past that we were to be at St. Cloud to dine with the Duchess of Kingston; Nothing was to hinder us from Coming in the Evening, but Alas! My good intention prov'd only a disturbance to your Neighbours, and just late enough to break the rest of all your servants and perhaps yourself. I came home with the disapointment of not having been able to Make My appologies in propria Persona. I hope you feel my distress, instead of accusing me, the One I deserve, the other not. [We shall] come to see you tomorrow Morning, [unless something] hapen to prevent it! Oh I wish you was well enough to come to us tomorrow to dinner and stay the Evening. I wont tell you what I shall have, Temptations now are too Cruel for your Situation. I only Mention my wish, if the executing them shou'd be possible, your Merit will be grater or my satisfaction the More flatter'd. I would Serve you and help you at dinner, and divert your pain after dinner by good Musik.

*Non so perche ho scritto tanto in una lingua che non m'appartiene, Mentre posso scriver nella Mia, che lei intende tanto bene, non ò pensato all'Amor proprio altrimenti non l'avrei fatto, in qualunque Modo Mi creda sempre sua obligatissima serva, e vera Amica,*

Maria Cosway[2]

**Translation**: I do not know why I have written so much in a language that does not belong to me, while I can write in mine, which you grasp so well. I have not thought selfishly, otherwise I would not have done it. Anyway, ever believe me to be your most obligatory servant, and true Friend.

Cosway's somewhat maternal concern with Jefferson's well-being relates to his right wrist, which he fractures probably on September 18. In his Memorandum Book, he enters "Pd. two Surgeons 12f" on that day.[3] L.G. Le Veillard writes to William Temple Franklin, "Day before yesterday, Mr. Jefferson dislocated his right wrist when attempting to jump over a fence in the Petit Cours. The wrist is in place all right but he has suffered a great deal and I do not see how he can write for another month."[4]

---

[2] "To Thomas Jefferson from Maria Cosway, [20 September 1786]," *Founders Online,* National Archives, https://founders.archives.gov/documents/Jefferson/01-10-02-0267. [Original source: *The Papers of Thomas Jefferson,* vol. 10, *22 June–31 December 1786,* ed. Julian P. Boyd. Princeton: Princeton University Press, 1954, pp. 393–394.]

[3] Thomas Jefferson, Memorandum Books, 1786," *Founders Online,* National Archives, https://founders.archives.gov/documents/Jefferson/02-01-02-0020, accessed 13 Sept. 2022.

[4] "Wrist Injury (1786)," *Thomas Jefferson Encyclopedia,* https://www.monticello.org/research-education/thomas-jefferson-encyclopedia/wrist-injury-1786/#fn-3, accessed 20 Aug. 2022.

The language in this initial missive is flirtatious more than friendly, as evident by her invitation for Jefferson to come to dine with them on September 21. She pledges to wait on him at dinner and then regale him with after-dinner music. Jefferson can only be ensorcelled. Yet Cosway signs off merely and unimpressively as "obliged servant and true Friend."

Jefferson writes his first letter to Cosway just over two weeks later (October 5), just prior to the Cosways leaving for London. He mentions to Maria that if the Cosways intend to leave Paris on that day, he cannot accompany them, since he has an appointment with a physician. He writes this letter with his left hand.

### "I must relinquish your charming company"
### TJ to MC, Paris, 5 Oct. 1786

I have passed the night in so much pain that I have not closed my eyes. It is with infinite regret therefore that I must relinquish your charming company for that of the Surgeon whom I have sent for to examine into the cause of this change. I am in hopes it is only the having rattled a little too freely over the pavement yesterday. If you do not go to day I shall still have the pleasure of seeing you again. If you do, god bless you wherever you go. Present me in the most friendly terms to Mr. Cosway, and let me hear of your safe arrival in England. Addio Addio.

Let me know if you do not go to day.[5]

Cosway receives Jefferson's letter and replies on the same day.

### "The charming days we have past together"
### MC to TJ, Paris, 5 Oct. 1786

I am very, very sorry indeed, and [remorseful?] for having been the Cause of your pains in the [night]; Why would you go? And why was I not more friendly to you and less to Myself by preventing your giving me the pleasure of your Company? You repeatedly said it wou'd do you no harm, I felt interested and did not insist. We shall go I believe this Morning, Nothing seems redy, but Mr. Cosway seems More dispos'd then I have seen him all this time. I shall write to

---

[5] "From Thomas Jefferson to Maria Cosway, [5 October 1786]," *Founders Online*, National Archives, https://founders.archives.gov/documents/Jefferson/01-10-02-0297. [Original source: *The Papers of Thomas Jefferson*, vol. 10, *22 June–31 December 1786*, ed. Julian P. Boyd. Princeton: Princeton University Press, 1954, pp. 431–433.]

you from England, it is impossible to be wanting to a person who has been so excesvely [sic] obliging. I dont attempt to make Compliments, they can be None for you, but I beg you will think us sensible to your kindness, and that it will be with infinite pleasure I shall remember the charming days we have past together, and shall long for next spring.

You will make me very happy, if you would send a line to the post restante at Antwerp, that I may know how you are.

Believe me dr: Sir your Most obliged affectionate servant,

Maria Cosway[6]


Four days later, Cosway writes again to Jefferson to ask about his wrist. The trip to Saint-Denis, as we shall see in Jefferson's second, enormously long letter, refers to Jefferson accompanying the Cosways via carriage from Paris to the pavilion at Saint-Denis, just a couple of kilometers north of Paris, as a means of being with Maria as long as he can. Maria's worry is that the trip will rattle Jefferson's wrist and cause him greater discomfort. At this point, Richard Cosway must know that Jefferson's interest in his wife is affectionate, not merely friendly. He likely perceives that Jefferson is an interloping pest, although a harmless interloping pest. It is unlikely that Richard Cosway feels threatened by Jefferson.


On October 9, Cosway writes a few sentences in an enclosure to a long letter from Trumbull.

### "I am adding a couple of lines..."

## MC to TJ, Antwerp, 9 Oct. 1786

*Aggiungo due versi per domandarle come sta, Spero il viaggio a St. Dennys non fu cagione che si ricordò di Noi con pena, riceverò presto notizia del suo perfetto ristabilimento, qual cosa darà infinito piacere alla sua sempre obligata ed affta. Amica.*

Maria Cosway

---

[6] "To Thomas Jefferson from Maria Cosway, [5 October 1786]," *Founders Online*, National Archives, https://founders.archives.gov/documents/Jefferson/01-10-02-0298. [Original source: *The Papers of Thomas Jefferson*, vol. 10, *22 June–31 December 1786*, ed. Julian P. Boyd. Princeton: Princeton University Press, 1954, p. 433.]

Mr. Cosway unisce i suoi ai miei Complimenti. Arrivammo qui domenica, tre ore doppo Mezza Notte.[7]

**Translation:** I am adding a couple of lines to ask you how you are. I hope the trip to St. Dennys did not cause you painfully to remember us. I shall soon receive news of your complete recovery, which will give infinite pleasure to your always obliged and affectionate Friend,

Maria Cosway.

Mr. Cosway adds his compliments to mine. We arrived here Sunday, three hours past midnight.

A few days after the departure of the Cosways, a disconsolate Jefferson pens what I take to be his most remarkable letter, revelatory of Jefferson's emotional self.[8]

### "Well, friend, you seem to be in a pretty trim"
### TJ to MC, Paris, 12 Oct. 1786

Madam:

Having performed the last sad office of handing you into your carriage at the Pavillon de St. Denis, and seen the wheels get actually into motion, I turned on my heel and walked, more dead than alive, to the opposite door, where my own was awaiting me. Mr. Danquerville was missing. He was sought for, found, and dragged down stairs. [We] were crammed into the carriage, like recruits for the Bastille, and not having [will]l enough to give orders to the coachman, he presumed Paris our destination, [then] drove off. After a considerable interval, silence was broke with a "je suis vraiment affligé du depart de ces bons gens."[9] This was the signal for a mutual confession [of dist]ress. We began immediately to talk of Mr. and Mrs. Cosway, of their goodness, their [virtues], their amability, and tho we spoke of nothing else, we seemed hardly to have entered into matter

---

[7] "To Thomas Jefferson from John Trumbull, with a Note from Maria Cosway, 9 October 1786," *Founders Online*, National Archives, https://founders.archives.gov/documents/Jefferson/01-10-02-0304. [Original source: *The Papers of Thomas Jefferson*, vol. 10, *22 June–31 December 1786*, ed. Julian P. Boyd. Princeton: Princeton University Press, 1954, pp. 438–441.]

[8] M. Andrew Holowchak, *Thomas Jefferson in Paris: The Ministry of a Virginian 'Looker on'* (Wilmington, DE: Vernon Press, 2022), chaps. 13 and 20.

[9] "I am much distressed by the departure of these good people."

when the coachman announced the rue St. Denis, and that we were opposite Mr. Danquerville's. He insisted on descending there and traversing a short passage to his lodgings. I was carried home. Seated by my fire side, solitary and sad, the following dialogue took place between my Head and my Heart.

**Head.** Well, friend, you seem to be in a pretty trim.

**Heart.** I am indeed the most wretched of all earthly beings. Overwhelmed with grief, every fibre of my frame distended beyond it's natural powers to bear, I would willingly meet whatever catastrophe should leave me no more to feel or to fear.

**Head.** These are the eternal consequences of your warmth and precipitation. This is one of the scrapes into which you are ever leading us. You confess your follies indeed: but still you hug and cherish them, and no reformation can be hoped, where there is no repentance.

**Heart.** Oh my friend! This is no moment to upbraid my foibles. I am rent into fragments by the force of my grief! If you have any balm, pour it into my wounds: if none, do not harrow them by new torments. Spare me in this awful moment! At any other I will attend with patience to your admonitions.

**Head.** On the contrary I never found that the moment of triumph with you was the moment of attention to my admonitions. While suffering under your follies you may perhaps be made sensible of them, but, the paroxysm over, you fancy it can never return. Harsh therefore as the medicine may be, it is my office to administer it. You will be pleased to remember that when our friend Trumbull used to be telling us of the merits and talents of these good people, I never ceased whispering to you that we had no occasion for new acquaintance; that the greater their merit and talents, the more dangerous their friendship to our tranquillity, because the regret at parting would be greater.

**Heart.** Accordingly, Sir, this acquaintance was not the consequence of my doings. It was one of your projects which threw us in the way of it. It was you, remember, and not I, who desired the meeting, at Legrand & Molinos. I never trouble myself with domes nor arches. The Halle aux bleds (Figure 1-1) might have rotted down before I should have gone to see it. But you, forsooth, who are eternally getting us to sleep with your diagrams and crotchets, must go and examine this wonderful piece of architecture. And when you had seen it, oh! it was the most superb thing on earth! What you had seen there was worth all you had yet seen in Paris! I thought so too. But I meant it of the lady and gentleman to whom we had been presented, and not of a parcel of sticks and chips put together in pens. You then, Sir, and not I, have been the cause of the present distress.

**Figure 1-1:** Nicolas-Marie-Joseph Chapuy, Halle aux Blés, 1838

Source: Wikipedia

**Head**. It would have been happy for you if my diagrams and crotchets had gotten you to sleep on that day, as you are pleased to say they eternally do. My visit to Legrand & Molinos had publick utility for it's object. A market is to be built in Richmond. What a commodious plan is that of Legrand & Molinos: especially if we put on it the noble dome of the Halle aux bleds. If such a bridge as they shewed us can be thrown across the Schuylkill at Philadelphia, the floating bridges taken up, and the navigation of that river opened, what a copious resource will be added, of wood and provisions, to warm and feed the poor of that city. While I was occupied with these objects, you were dilating with your new acquaintances, and contriving how to prevent a separation from them. Every soul of you had an engagement for the day. Yet all these were to be sacrificed, that you might dine together. Lying messengers were to be dispatched into every quarter of the city with apologies for your breach of engagement. You particularly had the effrontery [to] send word to the Dutchess Danville that, in the moment we were setting out to d[ine] with her, dispatches came to hand which required immediate attention. You [bid] me to invent a more ingenious excuse; but I knew you were getting into a scrape, and I would have nothing to do with it. Well, after dinner to St. Cloud, from St. Cloud to Ruggieri's, from Ruggieri to Krumfoltz, and if the day had been as long as a

Lapland summer day, you would still have contrived means, among you, to have filled it.

**Heart**. Oh! my dear friend, how you have revived me by recalling to my mind the transactions of that day! How well I remember them all, and that when I came home at night and looked back to the morning, it seemed to have been a month agone. Go on then, like a kind comforter, and paint to me the day we went to St. Germains. How beautiful was every object! the Port de Neuilly, the hills along the Seine, the rainbows of the machine of Marly, the terras of St. Germains, the chateaux, the gardens, the [statues] of Marly, the pavillon of Lucienne. Recollect too Madrid, Bagatelle, the King's garden, the Dessert. How grand the idea excited by the remains of such a column! The spiral staircase too was beautiful. Every moment was filled with something agreeable. The wheels of time moved on with a rapidity of which those of our carriage gave but a faint idea, and yet in the evening, when one took a retrospect of the day, what a mass of happiness had we travelled over! Retrace all those scenes to me, my good companion, and I will forgive the unkindness with which you were chiding me. The day we went to St. Germains was a little too warm, I think, was not it?

**Head**. Thou art the most incorrigible of all the beings that ever sinned! I reminded you of the follies of the first day, intending to deduce from thence some useful lessons for you, but instead of listening to these, you kindle at the recollection, you retrace the whole series with a fondness which shews you want nothing but the opportunity to act it over again. I often told you during it's course that you were imprudently engaging your affections under circumstances that must cost you a great deal of pain: that the persons indeed were of the greatest merit, possessing good sense, good humour, honest hearts, honest manners, and eminence in a lovely art: that the lady had moreover qualities and accomplishments, belonging to her sex, which might form a chapter apart for her: such as music, modesty, beauty, and that softness of disposition which is the ornament of her sex and charm of ours. But that all these considerations would increase the pang of separation: that their stay here was to be short: that you rack our whole system when you are parted from those you love, complaining that such a separation is worse than death, inasmuch as this ends our sufferings, whereas that only begins them: and that the separation would in this instance be the more severe as you would probably never see them again.

**Heart**. But they told me they would come back again the next year.

**Head**. But in the mean time see what you suffer: and their return too depends on so many circumstances that if you had a grain of prudence you would not count upon it. Upon the whole it is improbable and therefore you should abandon the idea of ever seeing them again.

**Heart.** May heaven abandon me if I do!

**Head.** Very well. Suppose then they come back. They are to stay here two months, and when these are expired, what is to follow? Perhaps you flatter yourself they may come to America?

**Heart.** God only knows what is to happen. I see nothing impossible in that supposition, and I see things wonderfully contrived sometimes to make us happy. Where could they find such objects as in America for the exercise of their enchanting art?. especially the lady, who paints landscape so inimitably. She wants only subjects worthy of immortality to render her pencil immortal. The Falling spring, the Cascade of Niagara, the Passage of the Potowmac thro the Blue mountains, the Natural bridge. It is worth a voiage across the Atlantic to see these objects; much more to paint, and make them, and thereby ourselves, known to all ages. And our own dear Monticello, where has nature spread so rich a mantle under the eye? mountains, forests, rocks, rivers. With what majesty do we there ride above the storms! How sublime to look down into the workhouse of nature, to see her clouds, hail, snow, rain, thunder, all fabricated at our feet! And the glorious Sun, when rising as if out of a distant water, just gilding the tops of the mountains, and giving life to all nature!

I hope in god no circumstance may ever make either seek an asylum from grief! With what sincere sympathy I would open every cell of my composition to receive the effusion of their woes! I would pour my tears into their wounds: and if a drop of balm could be found at the top of the Cordilleras, or at the remotest sources of the Missouri, I would go thither myself to seek and to bring it. Deeply practised in the school of affliction, the human heart knows no joy which I have not lost, no sorrow of which I have not drank! Fortune can present no grief of unknown form to me! Who then can so softly bind up the wound of another as he who has felt the same wound himself? But Heaven forbid they should ever know a sorrow!

Let us turn over another leaf, for this has distracted me.

**Head.** Well. Let us put this possibility to trial then on another point. When you consider the character which is given of our country by the lying newspapers of London, and their credulous copyers in other countries; when you reflect that all Europe is made to believe we are a lawless banditti, in a state of absolute anarchy, cutting one another's throats, and plundering without distinction, how can you expect that any reasonable creature would venture among us?

**Heart.** But you and I know that all this is false: that there is not a country on earth where there is greater tranquillity, where the laws are milder, or better obeyed: where every one is more attentive to his own business, or meddles less with that of others: where strangers are better received, more hospitably treated, and with a more sacred respect.

**Head**. True, you and I know this, but your friends do not know it.

**Heart**. But they are sensible people who think for themselves. They will ask of impartial foreigners who have been among us, whether they saw or heard on the spot any instances of anarchy. They will judge too that a people occupied as we are in opening rivers, digging navigable canals, making roads, building public schools, establishing academies, erecting busts and statues to our great men, protecting religious freedom, abolishing sanguinary punishments, reforming and improving our laws in general, they will judge I say for themselves whether these are not the occupations of a people at their ease, whether this is not better evidence of our true state than a London newspaper, hired to lie, and from which no truth can ever be extracted but by reversing everything it says.

**Head**. I did not begin this lecture my friend with a view to learn from you what America is doing. Let us return then to our point. I wished to make you sensible how imprudent it is to place your affections, without reserve, on objects you must so soon lose, and whose loss when it comes must cost you such severe pangs. Remember the last night. You knew your friends were to leave Paris to-day. This was enough to throw you into agonies. All night you tossed us from one side of the bed to the other. No sleep, no rest. The poor crippled wrist too, never left one moment in the same position, now up, now down, now here, now there; was it to be wondered at if all it's pains returned? The Surgeon then was to be called, and to be rated as an ignoramus because he could not devine the cause of this extraordinary change.

In fine, my friend, you must mend your manners. This is not a world to live at random in as you do. To avoid these eternal distresses, to which you are for ever exposing us, you must learn to look forward before you take a step which may interest our peace. Everything in this world is matter of calculation. Advance then with caution, the balance in your hand. Put into one scale the pleasures which any object may offer; but put fairly into the other the pains which are to follow, and see which preponderates. The making an acquaintance is not a matter of indifference. When a new one is proposed to you, view it all round. Consider what advantages it presents, and to what inconveniencies it may expose you. Do not bite at the bait of pleasure till you know there is no hook beneath it. The art of life is the art of avoiding pain: and he is the best pilot who steers clearest of the rocks and shoals with which it is beset. Pleasure is always before us; but misfortune is at our side: while running after that, this arrests us. The most effectual means of being secure against pain is to retire within ourselves, and to suffice for our own happiness. Those, which depend on ourselves, are the only pleasures a wise man will count on: for nothing is ours which another may deprive us of. Hence the inestimable value of intellectual pleasures. Ever in our power, always leading us to something new, never cloying, we ride, serene and sublime, above the concerns of this mortal world, contemplating truth and nature, matter and motion, the laws which bind up their existence, and that eternal being who made and bound them up by these laws. Let this be our employ. Leave the bustle and tumult of society to those who have not talents to occupy themselves without them. Friendship is but another name for an alliance with the follies and the misfortunes of others. Our own share of miseries is sufficient: why enter then as volunteers into those of another? Is there so little gall poured into our own cup that we must needs help to drink that of our neighbor? A friend dies or leaves us: we feel as if a limb was cut off. He is sick: we must watch over him, and participate of his pains. His fortune is shipwrecked: ours must be laid under contribution. He loses a child, a parent or a partner: we must mourn the loss as if it was our own.

**Heart**. And what more sublime delight than to mingle tears with one whom the hand of heaven hath smitten! To watch over the bed of sickness, and to beguile it's tedious and it's painful moments! To share our bread with one to whom misfortune has left none! This world abounds indeed with misery: to lighten it's burthen we must divide it with one another. But let us now try the virtues of your mathematical balance, and as you have put into one scale the burthens of friendship, let me put it's comforts into the other. When languishing then under disease, how grateful is the solace of our friends! How are we penetrated with their assiduities and attentions! How much are we supported by their encouragements and kind offices! When Heaven has taken from us some object of our love, how sweet is it to have a bosom whereon to recline our heads, and into which we may pour the torrent of our tears! Grief, with such a comfort, is almost a luxury! In a life where we are perpetually exposed to want and accident, yours is a wonderful proposition, to insulate ourselves, to retire from all aid, and to wrap ourselves in the mantle of self-sufficiency! For assuredly nobody will care for him who cares for nobody. But friendship is precious not only in the shade but in the sunshine of life: and thanks to a benevolent arrangement of things, the greater part of life is sunshine. I will recur for proof to the days we have lately passed. On these indeed the sun shone brightly! How gay did the face of nature appear! Hills, vallies, chateaux, gardens, rivers, every object wore it's liveliest hue! Whence did they borrow it? From the presence of our charming companion. They were pleasing, because she seemed pleased. Alone, the scene would have been dull and insipid: the participation of it with her gave it relish. Let the gloomy Monk, sequestered from the world, seek unsocial pleasures in the bottom of his cell! Let the sublimated philosopher grasp visionary happiness while pursuing phantoms dressed in the garb of truth! Their supreme wisdom is supreme folly: and they mistake for happiness the mere absence of pain. Had they ever felt the solid pleasure of one generous spasm of the heart, they would exchange for it all the frigid speculations of their lives, which you have been vaunting in such elevated terms. Believe me then, my friend, that that is a miserable arithmetic which would estimate friendship at nothing, or at less than nothing. Respect for you has induced me to enter into this discussion, and to hear principles uttered which I detest and abjure. Respect for myself now obliges me to recall you into the proper limits of your office. When nature assigned us the same habitation, she gave us over it a divided empire. To you she allotted the field of science, to me that of morals. When the circle is to be squared, or the orbit of a comet to be traced; when the arch of greatest strength, or the solid of least resistance is to be investigated, take you the problem: it is yours: nature has given me no cognisance of it. In like manner in denying to you the feelings of sympathy, of benevolence, of gratitude, of justice, of love, of friendship, she has excluded you from their controul. To these she has adapted the mechanism of the heart. Morals were too essential to the happiness of man to be risked on the incertain combinations of the head. She laid their foundation therefore in sentiment, not in science. That she gave to all, as necessary to all: this to a few only, as sufficing with a few. I know indeed that you pretend authority to the sovereign controul of our conduct in all it's parts: and a respect for your grave saws and maxims, a desire to do what is right, has sometimes induced me to conform to your counsels. A few facts however which I can readily recall to your memory, will suffice to prove to you that nature has not organised you for our moral direction. When the poor wearied souldier, whom we overtook at Chickahominy with his pack on his back, begged us to let him get up behind our chariot, you began to calculate that the road was full of souldiers, and that if all should be taken up our horses would fail in their journey. We drove on therefore. But soon becoming sensible you had made me do wrong, that tho we cannot relieve all the distressed we should relieve as many as we can, I turned about to take up the souldier; but he had entered a bye path, and was no more to be found: and from that moment to this I could never find him out to ask his forgiveness. Again, when the poor woman came to ask a charity in Philadelphia, you whispered that she looked like a drunkard, and that half a dollar was enough to give her for the ale-house. Those who want the dispositions to give, easily find reasons why they ought not to give. When I sought her out afterwards, and did what I should have done at first, you know that she employed the money immediately towards placing her child at school. If our country, when pressed with wrongs at the point of the bayonet, had been governed by it's heads instead of it's hearts, where should we have been now? hanging on a gallows as high as Haman's. You began to calculate and to compare wealth and numbers: we threw up a few pulsations of our warmest blood: we supplied enthusiasm against wealth and numbers: we put our existence to the hazard, when the hazard seemed against us, and we saved our country: justifying at the same time the ways of Providence, whose precept is to do always what is right, and leave the issue to him. In short, my friend, as far as my recollection serves me, I do not know that I ever did a good thing on your suggestion, or a dirty one without it. I do for ever then disclaim your interference in my province. Fill paper as you please with triangles and squares: try how many ways you can hang and combine them together. I shall never envy nor controul your sublime delights. But leave me to decide when and where friendships are to be contracted. You say I contract them at random, so you said the woman at Philadelphia was a drunkard. I receive no one into my esteem till I know they are worthy of it. Wealth, title, office, are no recommendations to my friendship. On the contrary great good qualities are requisite to make amends for their having wealth, title and office. You confess that in the present case I could not have made a worthier choice. You only object that I was so soon to lose them. We are not immortal ourselves, my friend; how can we expect our enjoiments to be so? We have no rose without it's thorn; no pleasure without alloy. It is the law of our existence; and we must acquiesce. It is the condition annexed to all our pleasures, not by us who receive, but by him who gives them. True, this condition is pressing cruelly on me at this moment. I feel more fit for death than life. But when I look back on the pleasures of which it is the consequence, I am conscious they were worth the price I am paying. Notwithstanding your endeavors too to damp my hopes, I comfort myself with expectations of their promised return. Hope is sweeter than despair, and they were too good to mean to deceive me. In the summer, said the gentleman; but in the spring, said the lady: and I should love her forever, were it only for that! Know then, my friend, that I have taken these good people into my bosom: that I have lodged them in the warmest cell I could find: that I love them, and will continue to love them thro life: that if fortune should dispose them on one side the globe, and me on the other, my affections shall pervade it's whole mass to reach them. Knowing then my determination, attempt not to disturb it. If you can at any time furnish matter for their amusement, it will be the office of a good neighbor to do it. I will in like manner seize any occasion which may offer to do the like good turn for you with Condorcet, Rittenhouse, Madison, La Cretelle, or any other of those worthy sons of science whom you so justly prize.

I thought this a favorable proposition whereon to rest the issue of the dialogue. So I put an end to it by calling for my nightcap. Methinks I hear you wish to heaven I had called a little sooner, and so spared you the ennui of such a tedious sermon. I did not interrupt them sooner because I was in a mood for hearing sermons. You too were the subject; and on such a thesis I never think the theme long; not even if I am to write it, and that slowly and awkwardly, as now, with the left hand. But that you may not be discoraged from a correspondence which begins so formidably, I will promise you on my honour that my future letters shall be of a reasonable length. I will even agree to express but half my esteem for you, for fear of cloying you with too full a dose. But, on your part, no curtailing. If your letters are as long as the bible, they will appear short to me. Only let them be brim full of affection. I shall read them with the dispositions with which Arlequin in les deux billets spelt the words 'je t'aime' and wished that the whole alphabet had entered into their composition.

We have had incessant rains since your departure. These make me fear for your health, as well as that you have had an uncomfortable journey. The same cause has prevented me from being able to give you any account of your friends here. This voiage to Fontainbleau will probably send the Count de Moutier and the Marquise de Brehan to America. Danquerville promised to visit me, but has not done it as yet. De latude comes sometimes to take family soupe with me, and entertains me with anecdotes of his five and thirty years imprisonment. How fertile is the mind of man which can make the Bastille and Dungeon of Vincennes yeild interesting anecdotes. You know this was for making four verses on Mme. de Pompadour. But I think you told me you did not know the verses. They were these. "Sans esprit, sans sentiment, Sans etre belle, ni neuve, En France on peut avoir le premier amant: Pompadour en est l'epreuve."[10] I have read the memoir of his three escapes. As to myself my health is good, except my wrist which mends slowly, and my mind which mends not at all, but broods constantly over your departure. The lateness of the season obliges me to decline my journey into the South of France. Present me in the most friendly terms to Mr. Maria, and receive me into your own recollection with a partiality and a warmth, proportioned, not to my own poor merit, but to the sentiments of sincere affection and esteem with which I have the honour to be, my dear Madam, your most obedient humble servant,

Th: Jefferson[11]

What are we to make of this letter?

I have elsewhere dilated on the lack of consensus concerning Jefferson's intendment in the secondary literature, so a detailed iteration of that scholarly analysis is unneeded.[12] A summary will suffice. Almost all see the letter as a debate[13] between Jefferson's intellect and his emotional self—mostly without recognition that the emotional self that Jefferson places on display is his moral self—and some see Jefferson's Head winning the debate[14]; others, Jefferson's

---

[10] "Without spirit, without feeling, / Without being beautiful, or new, / In France one can have the first lover: / Pompadour is the test."

[11] "From Thomas Jefferson to Maria Cosway, 12 October 1786," *Founders Online*, National Archives, https://founders.archives.gov/documents/Jefferson/01-10-02-0309. [Original source: *The Papers of Thomas Jefferson*, vol. 10, *22 June–31 December 1786*, ed. Julian P. Boyd. Princeton: Princeton University Press, 1954, pp. 443–455.]

[12] M. Andrew Holowchak, *Thomas Jefferson, Moralist* (Jefferson, IN: McFarland, 2017), chap. 1.

[13] Burnell writes, "The dialogue between his Head and his Heart was a debate about whether a friendship fated to end in separation should ever be undertaken." Carol Burnell, *Divided Affections*, 191.

[14] Joseph Ellis, *American Sphinx: The Character of Thomas Jefferson* (New York: Alfred A.

Heart.[15] Still others see a stalemate.[16] Some, like Peter Onuf, caution that we should not read too much into the letter, for the love letter, promises "to reveal everything" while in fact "revealing nothing."[17] Others, like Robert Dawidoff, state just that the letter is perplexing, though it must be acknowledged that Dawidoff tends to see as perplexing all that Jefferson writes.[18]

The letter is neither vacuous nor perplexing. It is the attempt of a man who is emotionally profuse and yet clumsy when it comes to displaying or conveying emotionality[19] to reveal his feelings for Cosway. Anticipating the probability of those feelings being unrequited, Jefferson arranges his thoughts into a sort of dialog or debate between his moral self, Heart, and his intellect, Head. When one studies his writings on moral sense and rationality, one sees that there is no possibility of open discussion of matters of the heart with the head or conversely. The realms of the two are distinct, and thus, intervention in the affairs of one by the other can only be abortive, even ruinous.[20]

Why, then, is there such an interactive discussion?

Jefferson is merely hedging his bets. If Cosway does not reciprocate his love for her, he can solace himself, in some measure, by stating through Head, "I knew that all along."

On the day after he pens his Head-and-Heart letter, Jefferson writes another letter to Cosway.

---

Knopf, 1998), 95; Andrew Burstein, *The Inner Jefferson* (Charlottesville: The University of Virginia Press, 1995), 94–96.

[15] Dumas Malone, *Jefferson and the Rights of Man* (Boston: Little, Brown and Company, 1951), 76–77, and Douglas L. Wilson, "Jefferson and the Republic of Letters," *Jeffersonian Legacies*, ed. Peter S. Onuf (Charlottesville: University Press of Virginia, 1991), 50–76.

[16] Daryl Hale, "Thomas Jefferson; Sublime or Sublimated Philosopher?" *International Social Science Review*, Vol. 72, Nos. 3 & 4, 2001, 81–82, and Lee Quinby, "Thomas Jefferson: The Virtue of Aesthetics and the Aesthetics of Virtue," *The American Historical Review*, Vol. 87, No. 2, 1982, 338.

[17] This is an astonishingly vacuous claim. Peter Onuf, *The Mind of Thomas Jefferson* (Charlottesville: University of Virginia Press, 2007), 3.

[18] E.g., Robert Dawidoff, "Man of Letters," *Thomas Jefferson: A Reference Biography*, ed. Merrill D. Peterson (New York: Charles Scribner's Sons, 1986), 193.

[19] M. Andrew Holowchak, *Thomas Jefferson: Psychobiography of an American Lion* (Hauppague, NY: Nova, 2019).

[20] M. Andrew Holowchak, "An 'Honest Heart' versus a 'Knowing Head'": The Myth of the Preeminency of Rationality in Jefferson's Notions of Man and Society," *The Elusive Thomas Jefferson: The Man behind the Myths*, eds. M. Andrew Holowchak and Brian Dotts (Jefferson, NC: McFarland, 2017), 5–23.

## "Little indeed, but better a little than none"
## TJ to MC, Paris, 13 Oct. 1786

My Dear Madam

Just as I had sealed the inclosed I received a letter of a good length, dated Antwerp, with your name at the bottom. I prepared myself for a feast. I read two or three sentences: looked again at the signature to see if I had not mistaken it. It was visibly yours. Read a sentence or two more. Diable! Spelt your name distinctly. There was not a letter of it omitted. Began to read again. In fine after reading a little and examining the signature, alternately, half a dozen times, I found that your name was to four lines only instead of four pages. I thank you for the four lines however because they prove you think of me. Little indeed, but better a little than none. To shew how much I think of you I send you the inclosed letter of three sheets of paper, being a history of the evening I parted with you. But how expect you should read a letter of three mortal sheets of paper? I will tell you. Divide it into six doses of half a sheet each, and every day, when the toilette begins, take a dose, that is to say, read half a sheet. By this means it will have the only merit it's length and dulness can aspire to, that of assisting your coëffeuse to procure you six good naps of sleep. I will even allow you twelve days to get through it, holding you rigorously to one condition only, that is, that at whatever hour you receive this, you do not break the seal of the inclosed till the next toilette. Of this injunction I require a sacred execution. I rest it on your friendship, and that in your first letter you tell me honestly whether you have honestly performed it.

I send you the song I promised. Bring me in return it's subject, Jours heureux! Were I a songster I should sing it all to these words "Dans ces lieux qu'elle tarde à se render"![21] Learn it I pray you, and sing it with feeling.

My right hand presents it's devoirs to you, and sees with great indignation the left supplanting it in a correspondence so much valued. You will know the first moment it can resume it's rights. The first exercise of them shall be addressed to you, as you had the first essay of it's rival. It will yet, however, be many a day. Present my esteem to Mr. Cosway, and believe me to be yours very affectionately,

Th: Jefferson[22]

---

[21] "She is slow to move in such places."
[22] "From Thomas Jefferson to Maria Cosway, 13 October 1786," *Founders Online*, National Archives, https://founders.archives.gov/documents/Jefferson/01-10-02-0313. [Original

The "letter of a good length" is from Trumbull (October 9), who informs Jefferson of the safe arrival of the Cosways at Antwerp. At the bottom of Trumbull's letter, there are, as Jefferson notes, four lines from Maria (see above, MC to TJ, 9 Oct. 1786). Jefferson, suffering saudade, expresses astonishment, as he has been certainly hoping for a missive from Cosway equally as long and equally as effusive as his letter from October 12. He has instead received "four lines only instead of four pages." It is a mortal blow to Jefferson, whose immense disappointment is evidenced by his penning three ungrammatical sentences, evidence of Jefferson's dismay: "Spelt your name distinctly,"; "Began to read again," and "Little indeed, but better a little than none." He solaces himself with the sentiment that he is at least in her thoughts. Jefferson then proffers instructions for her concerning how to read his effusive and long *billet doux*. She is to read the letter in six "doses," each taken at the start of a new day. He ends by stating that she will have the honor of receiving the first letter from him with his right hand when it is better. Jefferson is at the time, without question, reviewing, at least from memory, what are now the wise cautionary remarks of Head, throughout his love letter, to Heart about allowing oneself to love fully but without regard for loss.

Maria Cosway replies to Jefferson's *billet doux* in a letter dated October 30. It is necessary to study this reply with the same circumspection as Jefferson's love letter of October 12 to see whether Jefferson's love is reciprocated. That is something that scholars typically have not done.

### "Whatever I may say will appear trifling…"

## MC to TJ, London, 30 Oct. 1786

[I wish I] could answer the Dialogue! But I [my heart?] is invisable, and Mute, at this moment more than usual [it is] full or ready to burst with all the variety of Sentiments, wh[ich] a very feeling one is Capable of; sensible of My loss a[t] separating from the friends I left at Paris, I have hardly time to indulge a shamisly [shameless] tribute; but My thoughts Must be contrasted by the joy of Meeting my friends in London. It is an excess which Must tear to peices a human Mind, when felt. You seem to be Such a Master on this subject, that whatever I may say will appear trifling, not well express'd, faintly represented […] but felt. Your letter could employ me for some time, an hour to Consider every word, to every sentence I could write a volume, but I could wish that my selfishness was not reproching to Me, for with difficulty do I find a line but after

---

source: *The Papers of Thomas Jefferson*, vol. 10, *22 June–31 December 1786*, ed. Julian P. Boyd. Princeton: Princeton University Press, 1954, pp. 458–459.]

having admired it, I recolect some part concerns Me. Why do you say so Many kind things? Why present so many opportunities for my feeling undeserving of them, why not leave me a free consolation in admiring a friend, without the temptation [...] to my Vanity? I wish your heart [...] for it is too good. It expands to the Objects he [...] too Much of his own, and blinds the reality of its demerit.

*Ma cosa fo! Che scrivo tanto Inglese, Mentre posso scrivere nella Mia lingua, e rendermi un poco Meno imbrogliata, non sapevo cosa facevo, la vorrei riscrivere. Ma non gli voglio Mandare il primo foglio, le prime righe scritte al mio arrivo a Londra, siano le consequenze qual si voglia, Oh Sir se la Mia Corrispondenza valesse la sua quanto sarebbe perfetta! Non posso che esprimere la mia riconoscenza nella sua Amicizia. Mi perdoni se i suoi Comandi non furono ubbiditi, riguardo il tempo limitatomi per leggere la sua lettera Fu uno dei Miei primi piaceri il trovarla e non potei resistere all desiderio di leggerla subito, anche a costo di comettere un Atto di disabidienza.*

*Mi perdoni, il delitto lo Merita. Il nostro viaggio è stato felice, la Mia salute perfettamente ristabilita, il tempo buono eccettuato quei giorni precedenti alla nostra partenza da Parigi, la Compagnia di Mr. Trumbull [...] e piacevole. Ma Londra, l'ing[...] tra la nebbia e il fummo, la tristezza par [...]gra in ogni cuore, se si deve giudicare dalle fisonomie che s'incontrano; bisogna che ritorni il piu presto possibile alle mie Occupazioni per non sentire il rigore della Malinconia che inspira questo ingrato Clima, il ni Compagnia di amici che piaccino, esercitando un poco le belle arti, si può spesso evitar la tristezza, se qualcosa Manca alla perfetta felicità. Tutto è tranquillo, quieto, e tristo, non ci son Campane che suonano per annunziarci qualche festa, uffizzio, o gala, anche quando richiamano un Deprofundis s'accompagna con la speranza che quel anima passata a Miglior Vita gode quelle quiete beata, che il Mondo non accorda Mai a pieno: qui si sente la notte una voce ad ogni Ora che c'annunzia che è passata, ci soviene che non torna piu, e ci lascia spesso con la Mortificazione che l'abbiamo persa. Non ci son Monasteri ore son rinchiusi religiosi i quali a tutte le ore pregano per noi, e per chi non prega, quanti son persi, o nelle strade, o all gioco, nel vizzio, e l'Ozzio.*

*[...] come a Cominciato, a scriv[...] non saranno Mai abbastanza lunghe, quando [...] nelle sere lunghe del'inverno che li rimane qualche Momento non Occupato, lo Sacrifichi a Me, a Mandarmi Sue Nuove. Mi par Mill'Anni di ricevere una lettera dalla Man dritta, gli deve esser Molto scomodo scrivere con la Manca. Questo Sacrifizio Sarà ricevuto con tanta gratitudine, che dando fede alle promesse fatteci per le buone azzioni, invocherò per la sua ricompensa.*

*Mio Marito gli fa Mille Complimenti, la prego presentar i Nostri a Mr. Short, a Monr. D'ancherville quando lo vede. Non Mi scorderò Mai della sua attenzione per nai. Qualche volta Mentoveremo il Meditato giro l'anno venturo, se a Parigi,* se in Italia. Molte cose ponno impedirne l'esecuzione, Ma anche Maggior impossibilità Son State esercitate.

Accetti i Miei auguri per la sua salute e felicità e Mi creda la Sua Molto obligata ed affma. Amica.

Maria Cosway[23]

**Translation**: But what am I doing! I write so much in English, while I can write in my language, and make myself a little less unclear. I did not know what I was doing, and I would like to rewrite it [the part written in English?]. But do I not want to send you the first sheet, the first lines written on my arrival in London, whatever the consequences? O Sir, if my correspondence were the equal of yours, then how perfect things would be! I can only express my gratitude in your friendship. Forgive me if your injunctions, concerning how I should parse my time to read your letter, were not obeyed. It was one of my greatest pleasures to find your letter, and I could not resist the desire to read it at once, even at the cost of committing an act of disobedience. Forgive me, the crime deserves it.

Our journey was happy: my health perfectly restored, the weather good, except for those days before our departure from Paris, the company of Mr. Trumbull, amicable and pleasant. But in London, between the fog and the smoke, sadness seems predominant in every heart, if it is to be judged by the physiognomies that one encounters. I must return as soon as possible to my pasttimes so as not to feel the bite of the melancholy that permeates this unhappy climate. In the company of like-minded friends who practice a little the fine arts, you can often escape melancholy, though you will never find real happiness. Everything is tranquil, silent, and gloomy. There are no bells that peal to announce some feast, religious service, or gala. Even when they proclaim a *Deprofundis*, there is the hope in everyone that the soul of the departed has passed to better life and enjoys the sacred respite, which the world never fully allows. Here you hear at night a voice at every hour [i.e., the town crier] that announces that the hour has passed, and tells us that it never comes back, and leaves us with the mortification that we have forever lost it. There are no monasteries confining religious men, who at all hours pray for us; and for those who do not pray, how many are lost, or in the streets, or gambling—lost in vice and in idleness.

---

[23] "To Thomas Jefferson from Maria Cosway, [30 October 1786]," *Founders Online*, National Archives, https://founders.archives.gov/documents/Jefferson/01-10-02-0345. [Original source: *The Papers of Thomas Jefferson*, vol. 10, *22 June–31 December 1786*, ed. Julian P. Boyd. Princeton: Princeton University Press, 1954, pp. 494–496.]

When you begin another letter, it will never be long enough. When you suffer through the long evenings of the winter and you have some unoccupied moment, sacrifice it to me, and send me news of yourself. I shall wait even a hundred years to receive a letter from your right hand. It must be very painful for you to write with your left hand. That sacrifice I shall receive with such gratitude that, in keeping with the promises by God made to us for good actions, I shall invoke Him for your reward.

My husband gives you a thousand compliments. Please introduce our compliments to Mr. Short, to Monr. D'ancherville when you see them. I shall never forget the attention you paid to us while we were in Paris. I shall in time tell you of our planned visit next year to Paris or to Italy. Many things might foil the plans, but greater obstacles have been overcome.

Accept my best wishes for your health and happiness and believe me your very obliged and affectionate friend.

Maria Cosway

Much more than the four lines attached to Trumbull's long letter, this missive must have been a sockdolager to Jefferson. She begins by noting her sorrow at parting from her friends in Paris, but that is counterbalanced by her happiness by meeting again her friends in London. By implication, Jefferson is among her dearest friends, but he is just a friend, though much cherished.

Cosway distances herself in many ways: through self-deprecation, through switching to writing in Italian, through acknowledgment that Jefferson is her intellectual superior, and through turning to discussion of trifles. She begins. "Why do you say so many kind things?" She does not deserve them, and so Jefferson ought not to get emotionally involved. Then, Cosway continues in Italian, which Jefferson can read, though with difficulty, and which allows her to be "a little less involved." Third, she notes that her "correspondence" does not equal Jefferson's, as he is superior. Last, Cosway next turns to her voyage, her health, the weather, and Trumbull's companionship on her trip. Nowhere is there even any intimation that she might be harboring feelings of the sort Jefferson has for her.

I underscore the explicit expression of Cosway's melancholia, which she claims is brought on by London's dreary weather. In contrast to Paris, it is "tranquil, quiet and gloomy." She laments that the town crier announces each night another hour, but Cosway notes not the arrival of a new hour but the passing, never to return, of an old hour—a melancholy, pessimistic sentiment indeed.

There is not any hint in her reply to his *billet doux* of love for Jefferson. "Friend" and "friendship" only occur. The message to Jefferson is unambiguous, and he is crushed. He will not write to Cosway for over a month, and that long silence prompts the first of Cosway's several scolding letters, this one written wholly in Italian, a sure sign of her ire.

### "The pleasure which a sensitive soul feels in friendship"
### MC to TJ, London, 17 Nov. 1786

*Cosa vuol dir questo silenzio? O aspettata la posta con tanta Ansietà, ed ecco che ogni volta arriva senza apportarmi alcuna lettera da Parigi, veramente sono inquieta, temo che sia indisposizione o che il braccio stà peggio, penso a Mille cose alla volta fuor che i miei amici si sieno già scordati di me; se medita di farmi un altro gran regalo di una lunga lettera, la supplicherò di mandarmele piu corte, ma piu spesse. Non o piu pazzienza di aspettare e mi rischio di prender la penna senza esser sicura se devo lagnarmi, se devo rimproverare, se devo implorar la pazienza, raccontar la mia mortificazione, e inquietudini di questo disapuntamento, forse una lettera e per istrada, intanto mi lagnerò perche tanto ritarda ad arrivare. [...]ndo false, non senza [...] non apportano che delle consequenze che spesso ci fanno dispiacere, si suol pensare con sodisfazione alle ecclenti qualita delle persone per le quali si à della stima, della nostra felicità in poterne gustare il valore, e provare il piacere che un anima sensibile sente nell'-Amicizia, e cos'è la vita, privata di questo sentimento? Ma quando ci allontaniamo, passata la pena della separazione, si vive in continua inquietudine, non si riceve lettere si immagina mille disgrazzie, se qualche accidente accade, non si può accorrere con soccorso o consolazione, ne riceverne informazioni.*

*Il tempo qui e molto cattivo, malinconico, tristo. Molti de miei Amici, sono in campagna, sicche passo il mio tempo con quei pochi che ci sono, in dipingere, suonare l'arpa, il cimbalo e cantare, in questo modo lei mi dirà non si può che esser contenti, l'approvo anch'io, ma non so c'e qualcosa di tanto pesante in quest'aria, che tutto quel che fo mi par [...] dissipar la [noia...] ancora che per [...] che c'impone questo clima si starebbe [...] Night Thoughts, avanti al fuoco, e quando l'immaginazione e ben riscaldata, si potrebbe andar a raffreddarsi in un fieume. Non credo che neppur gli Dei sarebbero testimonij di questa stravaganza, tanto l'aria e cupa dalla nebbia e fummo, che impedisce i celesti abitatori di penetrar i loro sguardi fino alle debolezze umane di quest'isola.*

*Avrà inteso parlare dell sussurro che a fatto in questi. giorni Lord G. Gordon. La Morte della Principessa Amelia, per novità non e tempo di mandargliene, ne empierò un altra lettera.*

*Quando cominciai questa pensai di [non] dir che tre parole, ma insensibilmente sono arrivata fin qui senza neppur sapere cosa o detto, ma quando le donne cominciano a parlare e difficile il trattenerle, ancorche abbino l'avvertenza che dicono degli spropositi.*

*O veduto piu volte Mr. & Mrs. Paradise ed o il piacere di parlar di lei spesso con loro. Sarà sempre un infinita sodisfazione il mentovar il nome d'una persona che stimo, e questa la prova la sua vera amica,*

Maria Cosway[24]

**Translation**: What does this silence mean? I have waited for the mail with so much anxiety, and here every time it arrives without bringing me any letter from Paris, I become really agitated. I fear that you are indisposed or that your arm is worse. I can think of a thousand things at one time, but not of my friends having forgotten me and so soon after my return to England. If you aim to give me another large gift of a long letter, I beg you instead to increase their frequency and write shorter letters. I have not the patience to wait for another long letter. And so, I riskily take up my pen to write to you, but I know not whether I am to complain and to reproach, or to beg for patience and to tell you of my mortification and anxiety from not having got a letter. Maybe, a letter is on the way. In the meanwhile I shall complain because it is so late to arrive. Letters [from afar?] often bring only unpleasant news. We usually think with satisfaction of the excellent qualities of the people for whom we have esteem, of our happiness in being able to savor their value, and to experience the pleasure that a sensitive soul feels in friendship. What is life, if we are deprived of that pleasure? But when we part from our friends, the pain of separation leads to continuous anxiety. When we do not receive letters, we imagine a thousand misfortunes. If there occurs some accident, we cannot rush to help or console, for we get no news of the accident.

The weather here is extremely ill, melancholy, gloomy. Many of my friends are in the countryside, so I spend my time with those few that there are not. I paint, play the harp and the harpsichord, and I sing. In this way, you will say that I must be happy. That is so, but there is something so heavy in this air, that all that I do seems to be [mere boondoggling and boring?]. It is this climate that I suffer. [There are] Night Thoughts before a fire, and when the imagination is too much heated, one can cool off in a river. I do not believe that even the Gods could witness what goes on here, as the air is thick with

---

[24] "To Thomas Jefferson from Maria Cosway, [17 November 1786]," *Founders Online*, National Archives, https://founders.archives.gov/documents/Jefferson/01-10-02-0387. [Original source: *The Papers of Thomas Jefferson*, vol. 10, *22 June–31 December 1786*, ed. Julian P. Boyd. Princeton: Princeton University Press, 1954, pp. 538–540.].

gloomy fog, which prevents the heavenly inhabitants from seeing the human foibles of this island.

You must have heard about the sensational news these days about Lord G. Gordon and about the death of Princess Amelia. I have no time now to give you the details, so I shall tell you more in another letter.

When I started this letter, I aimed to say only three words, but I have without realization written so much without even knowing what I have written. When a woman begins to speak, it is difficult to hold back her, even if what she is saying is sheer nonsense.

I have seen Mr. & Mrs. Paradise several times and have had the pleasure of talking often about you with them. It will always be an infinite satisfaction the mention the name of a person whom I esteem, and this is felt by your true friend,

Maria Cosway

Cosway's scolding letter—she knows not whether to complain, to reprove, or to implore patience—seems like the sentiments of one in love and scorned. Yet there again appear only "friends" and "friendship." Jefferson is merely one of many persons for whom Cosway has esteem.

Why, then, is Cosway so upset if she is not in love with Jefferson?

Cosway is a coquette who thrives on the attention of males. She has, she knows, hooked Jefferson and she wishes never to release anyone she has hooked. There is a sort of safety in numbers. Moreover, poutiness is a technique that she uses to full effect with intimates. Consider for illustration this imploring letter to American-born painter James Northcote (see introduction), whom she implores, years later while in London, to come and dine with her.

> I will not be refused. I desire your company at dinner to-day. I am alone, alone. I dine after five. In the evening I will give you some superb music. I will sing, I will play, my organ will be in perfect order, I shall have other instruments to accompany me, greek beauties, and who can refuse? I will take no excuse. If you do not come to-day, expect everything from my fury. I will close the organ for ever to your ears.[25]

---

[25] Gerald Barnett, *Richard and Maria Cosway: A Biography* (Cambridge: Lutterworth Press, 1995), 144.

Jefferson replies to Cosway's scolding letter on November 19. It is now he who distances himself by writing with his painful right hand and that demands a short letter.

### "I write with pain"
## TJ to MC, Paris, 19 Nov. 1786

I begin, my dear Madam, to write a little with the right hand, and you are by promise, as well as by inclination entitled to it's first homage. But I write with pain and must be short. This is good news for you; for were the hand able to follow the effusions of the heart, that would cease to write only when this shall cease to beat. My first letter warned you of this danger. I became sensible myself of my transgression and promised to offend no more. Your goodness seems to have induced you to forgive, and even to flatter me. That was a great error. When sins are dear to us we are but too prone to slide into them again. The act of repentance itself is often sweetened with the thought that it clears our account for a repetition of the same sin. The friendly letter I have received from you might have been taken as a release from my promise: but you are saved by a cruel cramp in my hand which admonishes me in every line to condense my thoughts and words.

I made your excuses to Madame de Corny. She was as uneasy, as you had been, under the appearance of a failure in point of civility and respect. I knew the key to the riddle, and asked her on what day she had returned to town. She said on the 6th. of October. I told her you had left it on the 5th. Thus each stands excused in the eye of the other, and she will have the pleasure of seeing you in London. Nothing more will be necessary, for good people naturally grow together. I wish she could put me into her pocket, when she goes, or you, when she comes back.

Mercy, cramp! that twitch was too much. I am done, I am done.

*Adieu ma chere madame: je ne suis plus à moi. Faites mes compliments à Monsieur Cosway, assurez le de mon amitié, et daignez d'agreer vous meme l'hommage d'un sincere & tendre attachement. Encore adieu.*[26]

---

[26] "Farewell my dear madam: I am no longer myself. Make my compliments to Mr. Cosway, assure him of my friendship, and deign to accept yourself the tribute of one sincerely and tenderly attached. Farewell again." "From Thomas Jefferson to Maria Cosway, 19 November 1786," *Founders Online*, National Archives, https://founders.archives.gov/documents/Jefferson/01-10-02-0391. [Original source: *The Papers of Thomas Jefferson*, vol. 10, *22 June–31 December 1786*, ed. Julian P. Boyd. Princeton: Princeton University Press, 1954, pp. 542–543.]

True to his word, Jefferson pens the first letter that he writes with his right hand, still much paining him, to Cosway. Yet he teases her. His heart, says he, is suffuse with emotions for her and were his hand fully serviceable to the demands of his heart, she might be in receipt of another lengthy missive. Yet "I became sensible myself of my transgression and promised to offend no more," adds he, and that is clearly recognition that the battle of October 12 might have gone to Heart, but victory in the overall war is Head's.

Jefferson's reference to his "sins" is mouth honor to Cosway's Catholicism. Jefferson expressed his sin of logorrhea to Cosway on October 12. She has forgiven him, and with an unsullied soul, he is cleared for "a repetition of the same sin." Nonetheless, while the heart is willing, the hand is incapacitated. "Je ne suis plus à moi," sums Jefferson to show that he is physically unable to do what he wishes to do. The pain is too intense, or so Jefferson says. The pain is perhaps so intense that he cannot even sign the letter—at least, that is the impression he wishes to give unless it is a letter that he is sending by post. Such letters, he notes, are customarily opened on account of Jefferson's status, so if sent by post, he must disguise as much as he can, his letters. Yet if the letter is taken to Cosway by a messenger, then failure to sign the letter is merely a matter of teasing Cosway—to invoke a reaction of this sort: "So, I have become so insignificant that you deign not even to sign your letters to me!" Furthermore, Jefferson's right wrist is pained—"Mercy, cramp!"—and she is no longer to expect any long letters.

Yet Jefferson not only teases; he also tests. The letter holds out the hope that she can expect another "grandiloquent" letter if she sends him some hint of large affection for him. He did, after all, compose his *billet doux* entirely with his left hand, and Cosway can only be asking herself why the pain in his right hand prohibits him from continuing with his left hand.

It is generally overpassed by scholars that the time and effort it has taken to pen his *billet doux*, written by his left hand, is likely enormous and that time and effort are unquestionably measures of his deep feelings for her. Still, those feelings are not reciprocated and so, following Head, he now cannot invest himself fully in her, unless he wishes to drown in pain.

There is more here to say about Jefferson's fractured wrist. Jefferson, it must be noted, has injured his wrist in an effort to impress Cosway with his lissomeness, but the result has not been that of a polished Valentino but that of a bungling Keystone Kop. In his attempt to leap over the hedge of bushes, he has been tripped up by the hedge, falls hard on his right wrist, and thus sustains an injury that he will bear for life. Jefferson's pained wrist will ever be the recognition of that embarrassing event, and the embarrassment is decupled by his incapacity to win Maria's affection. In effect, the crippled wrist will serve as a lifelong reminder of that incapacity and of Cosway. Disability of the wrist will never signify disability of allure. There will ever be a physical reminder of his mental anguish.

Still, Jefferson, at this point, does not close the door on the possibility of something more than friendship. Yet, it is up to Maria to actualize that possibility.

Not having yet received Jefferson's cramped letter of November 19, Cosway pens another scolding letter, undated, to Jefferson. She is angry yet "full of esteem."

### "Every post-day I have waited anxiously"
## MC to TJ, London, 27 Nov. 1786

*Ho scritto due volte senza aver ricevuta una lettera da lei doppo la prima quale trovai all mio arrivo qui, e quale mi prometteva il piacere d'una piu frequente corrispondenza: Ogni giorno di posta o aspettato con inquietudine. Temo che il suo braccio sia peggio, ma anche questo non l'impedirebbe scrivermi. Prendo questa occasione di mandarli due linee per domandarli se a ricevute le mie lettere, per pregarla di mandarmi sue Nuove, e per ricordarli che sono piena di stima. Sua sincera ed affma. Amica,*

*Maria Cosway*[27]

**Translation**: I wrote twice without having received a letter from you after the first letter [with your right hand?] that I found on my arrival here, and which promised me the pleasure of a more frequent correspondence. Every day I await the mail with anxiety. I worry that your arm is worse, but knowing you, that would not stop you from writing to me. I take this opportunity to send you two lines to ask you if you have received my letters, to beg you to send me news of yourself and to remind you that I am full of esteem. Your sincere and affectionate friend,

Maria Cosway

Jefferson writes to Cosway on November 29. He proffers an explanation of his reticence to send personal letters through the post offices of France or England.

---

[27] "To Thomas Jefferson from Maria Cosway, [27 November 1786]," *Founders Online*, National Archives, https://founders.archives.gov/documents/Jefferson/01-10-02-0410. [Original source: *The Papers of Thomas Jefferson*, vol. 10, *22 June–31 December 1786*, ed. Julian P. Boyd. Princeton: Princeton University Press, 1954, p. 552.]

## "What a triumph for the head!"

## TJ to MC, Paris, 29 Nov. 1786

My letters which pass thro' the post office either of this country or of England being all opened, I send thro' that channel only such as are very indifferent in their nature. This is not the character, my dear madam of those I write to you. The breathings of a pure affection would be profaned by the eye of a Commis de la poste. I am obliged then to wait for private conveiances. I wrote to you so long ago as the 19th. of this month by a gentleman who was to go to London immediately. But he is not yet gone. Hence the delay of which you express yourself kindly sensible in yours of the 17th. instant. Could I write by the post, I should trouble you too often: for I am never happier than when I commit myself into dialogue with you, tho' it be but in imagination.

Heaven has submitted our being to some unkind laws. When those charming moments were present which I passed with you, they were clouded with the prospect that I was soon to lose you: and now, when I pass the same moments in review, I recollect nothing but the agreeable passages, and they fill me with regret. Thus, present joys are damped by a consciousness that they are passing from us; and past ones are only the subjects of sorrow and regret. I am determined when you come next not to admit the idea that we are ever to part again. But are you to come again? I dread the answer to this question, and that my poor heart has been duped by the fondness of it's wishes. What a triumph for the head!

God bless you! May your days be many and filled with sunshine! May your heart glow with warm affections, and all of them be gratified! Write to me often. Write affectionately, and freely, as I do to you. Say many kind things, and say them without reserve. They will be food for my soul. Adieu my dear friend!

P.S. No private conveiance occurring I must trust this thro' the post-office, disguising my seal and superscription.[28]

What is astonishing here is the optimism articulated in his letter of October 12—the optimism that is always so typical of Jefferson—has evanesced. Jefferson has adopted a dark Coswayan gloom. Heaven's laws are unkind. Recollection of the agreeable moments shared by the two is now a reason for

---

[28] "From Thomas Jefferson to Maria Cosway, 29 November 1786," *Founders Online*, National Archives, https://founders.archives.gov/documents/Jefferson/01-10-02-0416. [Original source: *The Papers of Thomas Jefferson*, vol. 10, *22 June–31 December 1786*, ed. Julian P. Boyd. Princeton: Princeton University Press, 1954, p. 555.]

regret, not joy. "Present joys are damped by a consciousness that they are passing from us; and past ones are only the subjects of sorrow and regret." What is worse is the thought of the two never again meeting, and Jefferson, upon entertaining the thought, banishes it from further consideration. It is, Jefferson freely admits, a triumph for Head.

The last letter of 1786 is penned by Jefferson on Christmas Eve.

**"I was so unlucky when very young, as to read the history of Fortunatus"**

## TJ to MC, Paris, 24 Dec. 1786

Paris, Dec. 24. 1786.

Yes, my dear Madam, I have received your three letters, and I am sure you must have thought hardly of me, when at the date of the last, you had not yet received one from me. But I had written two. The second, by the post, I hope you got about the beginning of this month: the first has been detained by the gentleman who was to have carried it. I suppose you will receive it with this.

I wish they had formed us like the birds of the air, able to fly where we please. I would have exchanged for this many of the boasted preeminencies of man. I was so unlucky when very young, as to read the history of Fortunatus. He had a cap of such virtues that when he put it on his head, and wished himself anywhere, he was there. I have been all my life sighing for this cap. Yet if I had it, I question if I should use it but once. I should wish myself with you, and not wish myself away again. *En attendant* the cap, I am always thinking of you. If I cannot be with you in reality, I will in imagination. But you say not a word of coming to Paris. Yet you were to come in the spring, and here is winter. It is time therefore you should be making your arrangements, packing your baggage &c. unless you really mean to disappoint us. If you do, I am determined not to suppose I am never to see you again. I will believe you intend to go to America, to draw the Natural bridge, the Peaks of Otter &c., that I shall meet you there, and visit with you all those grand scenes. I had rather be deceived, than live without hope. It is so sweet! It makes us ride so smoothly over the roughnesses of life. When clambering a mountain, we always hope the hill we are on is the last. But it is the next, and the next, and still the next. Think of me much, and warmly. Place me in your breast with those who you love most: and comfort me with your letters. *Addio la mia cara ed amabile amica!*

After finishing my letter, the gentleman who brought yours sent me a roll he had overlooked, which contained songs of your composition. I am sure they are charming, and I thank you for them. The first words which met my eye on opening them, are I fear, ominous. '*Qua l'attendo, e mai non viene.*'[29]

It is not happenstance that Jefferson pens this final letter of 1786 on Christmas Eve. Cosway is Catholic, and he thinks of her at this time of the year and longs to be with her, hence his reference to Fortunatus' Cap, which he would likely use but once—to be with Cosway. He bids her to consider planning for a trip to Paris in the summer of 1787. Jefferson entertains what he considers to be the likely eventuation of never again seeing Cosway. He falls back on hope, even if reason suggests that there is little reason for hope, yet the letter ends despairingly.

---

[29] "I wait here for him but he never comes." "From Thomas Jefferson to Maria Cosway, 24 December 1786," *Founders Online,* National Archives, https://founders.archives.gov/documents/Jefferson/01-10-02-0481. [Original source: *The Papers of Thomas Jefferson,* vol. 10, *22 June–31 December 1786,* ed. Julian P. Boyd. Princeton: Princeton University Press, 1954, pp. 627–628.]

Chapter II

# The Year 1787

Jefferson is busied after the Cosways return to London. Having brought with him to France his *Notes on the State of Virginia*, of which 200 copies were published in 1785 in Paris to be distributed cautiously by Jefferson, one copy falls into the hands of a bookseller, who arranges for a French translation, which is a horrid mutilation of Jefferson's text. Jefferson thus arranges for Abbé André Morellet to effect a better translation to supplant the first. The bookseller agrees, but Morellet's translation is, says Jefferson, "interverted, abridged, mutilated, and often reversing the sense of the original, [and] I found it a blotch of errors from beginning to end. I corrected some of the most material, and in that form, it was printed in French." The upshot is that Jefferson consents to have the book published by James Stockdale in English and made available to the general public, which has never been his wish.[1] Early in the year, he is also confronted with news of Shays' Rebellion, which has begun late in the summer of 1786. He pens several apologetic letters about the tragedy, which seems to those in and near Massachusetts to be the harbinger of another wholesale revolution. Later in the year, with the ratification of the Constitution on September 17, 1787, Jefferson preoccupies himself with consideration of the defects and virtues of the document.

When the Cosways' return to London after their trip to Paris, they resume their fashionable routine of entertaining high-society guests, visiting friends, resumption of work, and going to the theater in the evening. Helen Duprey Bullock writes of Richard's star at the time, "Cosway was not just a fashionable painter—he was the fashion." Though, pompous and vain, he is also admired, generous, and kindly.[2]

Angry at what she takes to be Jefferson's century-long silence, Maria Cosway begins the year with her third scolding letter. It is notable that Cosway pens seven letters in 1787; Jefferson, one. Cosway's first letter is wholly in Italian, a sure sign of her agitation.

---

[1] For more, see M. Andrew Holowchak, *Thomas Jefferson* Notes on the State of Virginia: *A Prolegomena* (Wilmington, DE: Vernon Press, 2023).
[2] Helen Duprey Bullock, *My Head and My Heart: A Little History of Thomas Jefferson and Maria Cosway* (New York: G.P. Putnam's Sons, 1945), 44.

## "In your last letter of a century ago…"
## MC to TJ, London, 1 Jan. 1787

*Amico*

*Ho aspettato con infinita ansietà la lunga lettera che m'annunziò, ma non so per qual delitto devo provar la penitenza di Tantalo, la credo ogni giorno vicina, ma quel giorno non arriva mai; nella sua ultima lettera d'un secolo passato mi dice aver ricevuta una mia lettera, ne o scritte fino tre, che mi ricordi, tutte dirette all' Banchiere secondo l'indirizzo che mi dette Mr. Trumbull. La perdita e mia, perche mi priva di quei momenti che sacrifica in leggere le mie lettere, mi richiamo per qualche instante alla sua memoria, e mi giustifica nel desiderio che o di farli i miei complimenti e di presentarli quelle attenzioni che lei tanto si merita per la sua compiacenza, ed amicizia per me; e quel che mi preme ancor di piu non mi dice come sta, se il suo braccio e guarito, se a ricevuto un libro di musica che gli mandai, tempo fà, […] Eccoli soggetti bastanti da impiegare due linee, che la conseguenza non è interessante che a me e che puo scrivere per farmi piacere.*

*Sono la peggio persona del mondo per mandar Novità sicchè non entrerò mai in quel soggetto; sono sensibile alla severità della stagione; a quest'ingrato clima, e alla malinconia del Paese; forse mi par piu severo adesso, doppo i mesi allegri che passai in Parigi ove tutto è allegro, sono suscettibile e tutto quel che mi sta attorno a gran potere a magnetisarmi. Se tengo piu dalla Natura d'un senso, e quello di malinconia, secondo gli oggetti che mi stanno attorno, si puo dissipare o accrescere. Tale e l'influenza sopra la suscettibilità.*

*Sono circondata da amabili Persone, Amici, e tutto quel che è lusinghevole, ma passo piu tempo in casa e posso dir che i piaceri vengono in traccia a me, perche non gli vado cercando altrove. Tutto il giorno dipingo, ed esercito la mia fantasia a tutto quel che indica, e tale e il piacere nella Pittura quando si a la libertà di seguire solo quando il desiderio c'inspira; la sera la passo generalmente in esercitarmi alla musica, e una amabile società rende l'armonia perfetta, ed ambi si uniscono a produrre il vero passatempo.*

*Non son stata all' Opera, ma sento che e cattiva, non vado mai all Teatro, ed o piu piacere in ricusare ogni altro divertimento e impegni, che di accettarli.*

*Ma cosa serve tutto questo preambolo, quando cominciai avevo intenzione di dir solo due parole, per confessar la verità voglio tenermi all' suo esempio; non voglio scancellare quel che o scritto perche sono riconoscente all' piacere che mi a procurato in conversar con lei, ma voglio esser crudele a me stessa e mortificarmi privandomi di continuar di più e finir con assicurarla che sono sempre con l'istessa stima ed affezione, Sua Um.ma: serva e vera amica,*

M.C.[3]

**Translation**: I have waited with infinite anxiety for the long letter that you promised me, but for what crime must I suffer the penance of Tantalus? When I believe that a letter is close every day, it never comes. In your last letter of a century ago, you tell me that you have received one letter of mine, that you have written three, which I recall, are all addressed to the Banker according to the address given to me by Mr. Trumbull. I am at a loss, as it deprives me of those moments that you sacrifice in reading my letters, as you recall me for a few moments to your memory, and as I am justified in the desire to send to you my compliments and to present you with those courtesies that you richly deserve for your kindness and friendship. What irks me most is that I do not know how you are, if your arm is healed, if you have received the book of music that I sent you, some time ago, [...] Here there are enough subjects for me to fill two lines, which are of interest to me, and that allows you to write to me as you please.

I am the worst person in the world to whom you send news, so I will never enter into that subject. I am sensitive to the vagaries of the seasons, to this ungrateful climate, and to the melancholy of the country. Perhaps it now seems more severe, on account of the cheerful months I spent in Paris, where everything is cheerful. I am susceptible to changes of climate and everything around me has great power to influence me. If I am disposed by Nature toward any one feeling, it is that of melancholy, and that varies according to the objects around me: It can dissipate or increase. Such is the influence of my susceptibility.

I am surrounded by lovable people, friends, and all things flattering, but I spend my time at home, and I can say that pleasures come to me, because I do not go looking for them. All day I paint, and I exercise my imagination to all that comes to mind, and such is my pleasure in painting when you give yourself the freedom to paint when inspired by passion. In the evening, I generally practice music, and that, along with pleasant society, makes for me perfect harmony. They blend together to produce genuine pastime.

---

[3] "To Thomas Jefferson from Maria Cosway, 1 January 1787," Founders Online, National Archives, https://founders.archives.gov/documents/Jefferson/01-11-02-0001. [Original source: The Papers of Thomas Jefferson, vol. 11, 1 January–6 August 1787, ed. Julian P. Boyd. Princeton: Princeton University Press, 1955, pp. 3–4.]

I have not been to the Opera, but I feel that it is bad. I never go to the Theater, and I take more pleasure in declining all other amusements and commitments, than in accepting them.

But what is the use of all this preamble? When I began to write, I intended to write two lines, and to confess the truth, I want to be consistent with my intention. Yet I do not want to excise what I have written because I am grateful for the pleasure that I have derived in conversation with you, but I want to be cruel to myself and mortify myself by depriving myself of writing further. I end by assuring you that I am always with the same esteem and affection, Your humble servant and true friend,

M.C.

The letter handsomely epitomizes Cosway's manic-depressive personality. Her anxiety is "infinite," she suffers like Tantalus, and Jefferson's last letter was 100 years ago. She writes of her sensitivity to seasonal fluctuations and her melancholy disposition, which is intensified or diminished "according to the objects which surround me," and she suffers more because her days in Paris have been gay. To make matters worse, she has fallen into a leaden regularity. She shuns gaiety—"I take more pleasure in declining all other amusements and commitments"—and paints all day and practices music at night. There is catharsis in writing to Jefferson, but she even disallows herself too much of that pleasure, and so she prematurely ends her letter, or so says she.

Receiving nothing from Jefferson, Cosway writes again in the middle of February. It is again a scolding, "reproaching" letter and one of considerable length.

### "An enfant gatée"

## MC to TJ, London, 15 Feb. 1787

I have the pleasure of receiving two [of your letters, and though th]ey are very short [Nov. 29 and Dec. 24], I must content Myself, and lament Much fo[r the] reason that deprivd Me of their usual length. I must confess that the begining of your corrispondence has made Me an *enfant gatée*.[4] I shall never recover to be reasonable in My expectations, and shall feel disapointed whenever your letters are not as long as the first was. Thus you are the occasion of a continual reproching disposition in Me. It is a disagreable One. It will teaze you to a hatread towards Me, notwithstanding your partiality you have had for Me till

---

[4] "A spoiled child."

now. Nothing disobliges More than a disatisfied Mind, and thou' my fault is occasion'd by yourself you will be the most distant to allow it. I trust that your friendship would wish to see Me perfect, and Mine to be so, but diffects [defects] are, or are not, Most conspicuous according to the feel we have about the Objects which Mislead them. We may be apt to feel our own [defects], as to discover them in others, and in both, one of the humane weakness we are subject to. [This peculiarity of ch]aracter, we both possess it, you to [the defect of?] thought, I for suffering patiently those not bestow'd [or be]gruje [begrudged] them, and silence My pretensions with due consciousness; I feel at present an inclination to Make you an endless letter but have not yet determin'd what subject to begin with. Shall I continue this reproching stile; quote all the what's, and why's, out of Jeremias's lamentations, then present you with some outlines of Job for Consolation? Of all the torments, temptations, and weariness, the female has always been the principal and most powerfull object, and this is to be the most fear'd by you at present, from my pen. Are you to be painted in future ages sitting solitary and sad, on the beautifull Monticello tormented by the shadow of a woman who will present you a deform'd rod, twisted and broken, instead of the emblematical instrument belonging to the Muses, held by Genius, inspired by wit, from which all that is pleasing, beautifull and happy can be describ'd to entertain, and satisfy a Mind capable of investigating every Minutia of a lively immagination and interesting descriptions[?]

[I wri]t[e] this in Memoria of the Many pages [you have written in response to the scr]awls adress'd to you by One who has only a good intention to [ask for apolo]gies for such long insipid Chit chat, that follows more the dictates of her own pleasure, than the feeling of understanding: Allegories are allways very far fecht. I don't like to follow the subject, though I Might find something to explain My Ideas. Supose I turn to relate to you the debats of Parlement? Was I a good politition I could entertain you Much. What do you think of a famous speach Sheridan has made which lasted five hours? which has astonished every body which has Made the subject of conversation and admiration of the whole Town. Nothing has been taulk'd of for Many days but his Speach. The Whole House applauded him at the Moment. Each Member Complimented him when they rouse. Pitt Made him the highest encomioms, and only poor Mr. Hastings sufferd for the power of his eloquence; all went against him, though nothing can be decided yet. Mr. H. was with Mr. Cosway at the very Moment [that Sheridan's speech was] going on. He seemd perfectly easy, talk[ing about a variet]y of subjects with great tranquility and cheerfulness. The second day he was the same, but on the third seem'd very Much affected and agitated. All his friends give him the greatest Character of humanity, generosity and feelings, amiable in his Maner. He seems in short totaly different from the disposition of cruelty they accuse him of.

From Parlementary discussions it is time to tell you I have ben reading with great pleasure your description of America. It is wrot by *you*, but Nature represents all the scenes to Me in reality. Therefore dont take any thing on yourself. I must refer to your Name to Make it the More valuable to Me but she is your rival, you her usurper. Oh how I wish My self in those delightful places! Those enchanted Grotto's! Those Magnificent Mountains rivers, &c. &c! Why am I not a Man that I could sett out immediatly and satisfy My Curiosity, indulge My sight with wonders!

[…] in Lond[on there have been man]y little parties. I have [been to not many of] them. I am grown so excessively indolent, that I [refuse not go] out for Months together. All the Morning I paint whatev[er] presents it self most pleasing to Me. Some times I have beautifull Objects to paint from and add historical Characters to Make them More interesting. Female and infantine beauty is the Most perfect Object to see. Sometimes I indulge More Malincholy subjects. History rappresents her self sometimes in the horrid, in the grand, the sublime, the sentimental, the pathetik. I attempt, I exercise and end by being witness of My own dissapointment and incapacity of executing, the Poet, the Historian, or my own conceptions of immagination. Thus the Mornings are spent regretting they are not longer, to have More time to attempt again in Search of better success, or thinking they have been too long and have afforded me Many Moments of uneasiness, anxiety and a testimony of my not being able to do any thing.

[In the eveni]ng, I practice and [play] Music and then I am Much [entertained by] the first Professors who come very often to play, every evening Something new, and all perfect in their different kind. And to add to Compleat the pleasure a small society of agreable friends frequently Come to see me. In this Manner you see that I am More attached to My home, than going in search of amusement out, where nothing but crowded assemblies, uncomfortable heat, and not the least pleasure in Meeting every body, not being able to enjoy any conversation. The Operas are very bad tho' Rubinelli and Madme. Mosa are the first singers, the danceres are very bad. All this I say from report as I have not been yet.

Pray tell me Something about Madme. de Polignac. They make a great deal about it here. We hardly hear any thing else, and the stories are so different from one another that it [is] impossible to guess the real one. She is expected in England. I send this letter by a gentleman whom I think you will like. He is a Spaniard. I am partial to that Nation as I know several that are very agreable. He is going to Paris Secretary of Ambassy [of the] Court. He has travel'd Mu[ch....]

If I should be happy enough to come again in the Sum[mer to] Paris I hope we shall pass many agreable days. I am in a Millio[n] fears about it. Mr. Cosway still keeps his intention, but how man[y] chances from our inclinations to the execution of our will! Poor D'Ancarville has been very ill. I received a very long letter from him appointing himself My *Corrispondant* at Paris. I know a Gentleman who has banished My faith in this occasion for he flatter'd me with hopes which I have seen fail. However I have accepted his offer. I shall see if I find a second disapointment.

Is it not time to finish My letter? Perhaps I should go on but I must send this to the gentleman who is to take it.

I hope you are quite well by this time, that your hand will tell me so by a line. I must be reasonable, but give me leave to remind you how Much pleasure you will give, to remember Sometimes with friendship One who will be sensible and gratfull of it as is yours Sincerely,

Maria Cosway[5]

Cosway admits to this letter, "that follows more the dictates of her own pleasure," being excessively skimble-scamble, although all her letters suffer from that defect. She not only reproaches Jefferson, but she also attacks him. He is not to underestimate the lure and power of "the female." She warns, "Are you to be painted in future ages sitting solitary and sad, on the beautifull Monticello tormented by the shadow of a woman who will present you a deform'd rod, twisted and broken, instead of the emblematical instrument belonging to the Muses, held by Genius, inspired by wit, from which all that is pleasing, beautifull and happy can be describ'd to entertain, and satisfy a Mind capable of investigating every Minutia of a lively immagination and interesting descriptions[?]"

Cosway admits that Jefferson's *billet doux* has made her an *enfant gatée*. She will never be dissatisfied with Jefferson unless all his future letters are of the length and sort of that letter. The length of her letter is certainly a lure to encourage Jefferson to craft another inordinately extensive love letter.

There are a few lines to show Jefferson that Cosway has been reading his *Notes on Virginia*. Were she a man, says she, she would immediately set out for the New World.

Cosway again notes that she seldom attends parties and shuns opera and the theater. Her time she spends painting, and she indulges in "More Malincholy subjects" when her mood is downcast, and it is seldom not downcast. "History

---

[5] "To Thomas Jefferson from Maria Cosway, 15 February 1787," *Founders Online*, National Archives, https://founders.archives.gov/documents/Jefferson/01-11-02-0154. [Original source: *The Papers of Thomas Jefferson*, vol. 11, *1 January–6 August 1787*, ed. Julian P. Boyd. Princeton: Princeton University Press, 1955, pp. 148–151.]

rappresents her self sometimes in the horrid, in the grand, the sublime, the sentimental, the pathetik."

Jefferson ends his "century-long" silence with a letter on the first of July. His long silence has been due to a lengthy trip to Southern France and Northern Italy from February 28 to June 10. One of the benefits of being minister plenipotentiary to France is that it affords Jefferson much free time, though when there is work to do, his time is not his time.[6]

### "I was born to lose every thing I love"

## TJ to MC, Paris, 1 July 1787

You conclude, Madam, from my long silence that I am gone to the other world. Nothing else would have prevented my writing to you so long. I have not thought of you the less. But I took a peep only into Elysium. I entered it at one door, and came out at another, having seen, as I past, only Turin, Milan, and Genoa. I calculated the hours it would have taken to carry me on to Rome. But they were exactly so many more than I had to spare. Was not this provoking? In thirty hours from Milan I could have been at the espousals of the Doge and Adriatic. But I am born to lose every thing I love. Why were you not with me? So many enchanting scenes which only wanted your pencil to consecrate them to fame. Whenever you go to Italy you must pass at the Col de Tende. You may go in your chariot in full trot from Nice to Turin, as if there were no mountain. But have your pallet and pencil ready: for you will be sure to stop in the passage, at the chateau de Saorgio. Imagine to yourself, madam, a castle and village hanging to a cloud in front. On one hand a mountain cloven through to let pass a gurgling stream; on the other a river, over which is thrown a magnificent bridge; the whole formed into a bason [sic], it's sides shagged with rocks, olive trees, vines, herds, &c. I insist on your painting it.

How do you do? How have you done? and when are you coming here? If not at all, what did you ever come for? Only to make people miserable at losing you. Consider that you are but 4. days from Paris. If you come by the way of St. Omers, which is but two posts further, you will see a new and beautiful country. Come then, my dear Madam, and we will breakfast every day á l'Angloise, hide away to the Desert, dine under the bowers of Marly, and forget that we are ever to part again. I received, in the moment of my departure your favor of Feb. 15. and long to receive another: but lengthy, warm, and flowing from the heart, as

---

[6] For more on the trip, see M. Andrew Holowchak, *Thomas Jefferson in Paris: The Ministry of a Virginian "Looker-on"* (Wilmington, DE: Vernon Press, 2022), chap. 17.

do the sentiments of friendship & esteem with which I have the honor to be, dear Madam, your affectionate friend & servant,

Th: Jefferson[7]

This letter finds Jefferson both in a saturnine and peppy mood. His recollections of his trip are reasons for the lively prose; that Cosway was not with him and the thought that she might not return to Paris in 1787 are reasons for melancholy. Jefferson has clearly often thought of Cosway during his trip.

Cosway replies by penning another angry letter written on a small sheet of paper to keep her from profuseness. The letter, however, is profuse, somewhat so. As is her wont, she slips into the use of Italian when irritated.

### "It seems a dream to have been there"
## MC to TJ, London, 9 July 1787

Do you deserve a long letter, My dear friend? No, certainly not, and to avoid temptation, I take a small sheet of paper; Conversing with you, would break on Any resolution. I am determind to prevent it. How long you like to keep your friends in anxiety!

How Many Months was you without writing to Me? And you felt no remorse?

I was glad to know you was well, sure of your being much engaged and diverted, and had only to lament I was not a Castle hanging to cloud, a stream, a village, a stone on the pavement of Turin, Milan, and Genoa &c. &c. No! I enter'd in the Calculation of hours that prevented you from visiting Rome. I am not sure if I had any share in the *provoking part;* oh! if I had been a shadow of this *Elysium* of yours! how you would have been tormented! I must excuse you a little, since you tell me you thought of me, and Italy was your Object. You advise me to go this beautifful tour, do you forget *che fu la Mia Cuna, che sull' limpido Corrente del' Arno ricevei la Vita? Che all Tevere fu il mio primo viaggio. Che Turino M'arrestò Nella Mia strada a Londra? Contutto ciò vorrei che M'avesse dato una pià lunga relazione dell' Suo Viaggio; le Sue osservazioni mi piacciono, il Suo gusto e buono, le Sue lettere m'interessano, ed aspettavo quasi in dritto, che mi avrebbe scritte tante pagine, quanti giorni fu assente. Specialmente avendo tanti suggetti, se pure qualcosa può Mancare per ajutare*

---

[7] "From Thomas Jefferson to Maria Cosway, 1 July 1787," *Founders Online*, National Archives, https://founders.archives.gov/documents/Jefferson/01-11-02-0435. [Original source: *The Papers of Thomas Jefferson*, vol. 11, *1 January–6 August 1787*, ed. Julian P. Boyd. Princeton: Princeton University Press, 1955, pp. 519–520.].

*la Sua immaginazione, Ma renderebbeli lo Scrivermi più piacevole, Mentre, ripass[er]ebbe con la penna quei luoghi che gli dettero tanto piacere. Sono veramente Mortificata, niente potrebbe pacificarmi, che queste linee sono Sue, ed allora, Non Misuro la scarsezza delle linee Ma il piacere che M'apporttano.*

*Non so se verremo a Parigi quest' anno, temo di No, Mio Marito Comincia a dubitarne, giusto al tempo che dovrebbe prepararsi per partire; Non puol credere quanto Mi dispiace quest' incertezza, ò tutto da temere contro il Mio desiderio. Perche promettere? Perche lusingarmi? Mi par Un sogno d' esservi stato, e lo desidero adesso realizzato, per l' impressione che mi lasciò. Almeno dia la Consolazione di ricevere nuove di un luogo che tanto M'interessa. Mi dica che Comedie ci sono nuove e buone, che Opere, che produzioni d'arti &c. &c. tutto quelche può indurlo a scrivermi delle lunghe lettere. Mi guastò sull' principio della nostra corrispondenza, glielo dissi, non a piu seguitato.*

*Ho avuto il piacere finalmente di vedere Madme. de Corny Mi piace assai, e molto amabile, e graziosa. Mi rincresce non averla Conosciuta prima.*

*Non. Mi dice niente ne della Sua Salute, ne del Suo braccio, bravo bravissimo.*

*Mi dispiace che non o occasione di vedere la Sua Figlia che mi dicono e qui presentemente. Non Conosco Mrs. Adams, e mi lusingo che se lei avessi creduto che io potessi esserle utile in qualsiasi Cosa, avrebbe reso giustizia all' Mio desiderio di Mostrarli in ogni occasione quanto son riconoscente della Sua amicizia per la Sua piu Aff.ma ed Ob.ma Servant,*

*Maria Cosway*

*Mio Marito à l'onore di presentarli i Suoi ossequi.*

Will you excuse the liberty I take in troubling you with these letters and a parcel. I shall be much obliged to you if you will be so good to send them. I dont know where the Duchess of Kingston leaves [lives] as I used to send to her at Calais and have been told she has removed from her House in Paris.[8]

**Translation**: [Do you forget] that that was my cradle, and on the clear current of the Arno I received Life? Do you forget that the Tiber was my first trip? Do you forget that Turin stopped me on my way to London? Such things noted, I wish

---

[8] "To Thomas Jefferson from Maria Cosway, 9 July 1787," Founders Online, National Archives, https://founders.archives.gov/documents/Jefferson/01-11-02-0484. [Original source: The Papers of Thomas Jefferson, vol. 11, 1 January–6 August 1787, ed. Julian P. Boyd. Princeton: Princeton University Press, 1955, pp. 567–569.]

you would have given me a longer report of your trip [through France]. I like your observations, your taste is good, your letters interest me, and I expected almost by right, that you would write me so many pages as the number of days you were gone. Especially since you had so many things to observe, if even something might have been missing, it would have been more pleasant for you to write to me to pique your imagination, while you were reviewing with your pen those places that gave you so much pleasure. Yet I am truly mortified, nothing can pacify me, that these [all-too-few] lines are yours, but then, I do not measure the scarcity of the lines but the pleasure they bring me.

I do not know if we shall come to Paris this year. I am afraid that we shall not. My husband begins to doubt it, and that is just at the time he should be preparing to leave. You cannot believe how sorry I am for this uncertainty. It is a fear that contradicts my desire. Why promise? Why lead me to hope? My having been to Paris now seems like a dream, but I wish now that it [a trip in 1787] should be fulfilled, because of the impression my prior trip left me. At least offer me the consolation of receiving news from you of a place that interests me so much. Tell me what Comedies are new and good, what Operas, what works of arts &c. &c., all such things that can induce you to write me long letters. You spoiled me at the start of our letter-writing, as I have often told you, and you no longer spoil me.

I finally had the pleasure of seeing Madme. de Corny. I like her very much. She is very lovable, and lovely. I regret not having met her sooner.

You tell me nothing about your health, nothing about your arm—*bravo bravissimo*.

I am sorry that I have not the occasion to see your daughter whom they tell me is presently here. I do not know Mrs. Adams, and I flatter myself that if you had believed that I could be useful to you in anything, you would have done justice to my desire to show them at every opportunity how grateful I am for your friendship for your most affectionate and obedient servant,

Maria Cosway


My husband has the honor to present His respects to you.


Cosway is clearly not solaced by Jefferson's explanation of his lengthy silence. "if I had been a shadow of this *Elysium* of yours! how you would have been tormented!" She adds that "by right" she deserves one page for each day of Jefferson's travels. "You spoiled me at the start of our letter-writing, as I have often told you, and you no longer spoil me." She includes the sentiment that it is doubtful that she will come to Paris in the summer.

Cosway's artistic time is well spent. In 1787, she has five pictures that are on display at the Academy in London: *Young Cybele with Two Nymphs*, *Young Bacchus* (Figure 2-1), *An Enchantress* (a lady with two children), *Psyche*, and *Portrait of a Lady* (self-portrait). Her renewed success is certainly due to artistic restraint. Cosway turns to portraits, more befitting a woman, not historical scenes. Of her depiction of Countess of Jersey, *St. James Chronicle* says, "The productions of Maria are much superior to those of her husband."[9]

Yet Cosway does come in the summer, on August 28, but without her husband. She stays with Princess Aleskandra Lubormirska, a Polish widow related to Poland's king. The princess' house is far from Jefferson's residence on the western outskirts of Paris, and that makes it difficult to communicate and visit. It is unclear whether Cosway has any choice in her residency. If so, then the choice of staying with the princess is a decision to be far from Jefferson.

**Figure 2-1:** Maria Cosway, *Young Bacchus*, 1787

Source: Gerald Barnett, *Richard and Maria Cosway: A Biography* (Cambridge: Lutterworth Press, 1995).

---

[9] Carol Burnell, *Divided Affections: The Extraordinary Life of Maria Cosway: Celebrity Artist and Thomas Jefferson's Impossible Love* (London: Column House, 2007), 205.

Cosway and Jefferson will see very little of each other in her three months in Paris. Jefferson explains the misfortune to John Trumbull (13 Nov. 1817): "A fatality has attended my wishes, and her and my endeavors to see one another more since she has been here. From the mere effect of chance, she has happened to be from home several times when I have called on her, and I, when she has called on me. I hope for better luck hereafter."[10] Jefferson is clearly rationalizing. Two people who want to be together will find ways of being together. Cosway is avoiding Jefferson. Jefferson, deep down, knows that. He refuses to acknowledge what he subconsciously knows.

Cosway is to leave Paris early in December, and Jefferson plans an elaborate dinner party in her honor prior to her departure. Cosway responds to his invitation.

### "If that could soften My regret…"
## MC to TJ, London, 1 Dec.(?) 1787

My dear sir

Why will you Make such a great dinner? I had told the Princess of the pleasure I intended My self tomorrow and she seemd very glad to go with me, but had not thought of any body else; to begin by Mr: d'Hancarville he is very sorry not to be able to wait on you as he has been particularly engaged for some time past. Mr: St: Andre I shall see this Evening. Monr: Nimscevik accepts with pleasure your kind invitation, Count Btorki is not here, but I shall deliver to him also your invitation. If my inclination had been your law I should have had the pleasure of seeing you More then I have. I have felt the *loss* with displeasure, but on My return to England when I calculate the time I have been in Paris, I shall not beleave it possible. At least if that could soften My regret, I shall encourage My immagination to favor Me. Addieu My dear friend, let me beg of you to preserve Me that name, I shall endeavour to deserve it: & all the Gods will bless us.

I hope Mr. Short will not be out as his usual when I have the pleasure to come to you.[11]

---

[10] "Thomas Jefferson to John Trumbull, 10 January 1817," Founders Online, National Archives, https://founders.archives.gov/documents/Jefferson/03-10-02-0508. [Original source: The Papers of Thomas Jefferson, Retirement Series, vol. 10, May 1816 to 18 January 1817, ed. J. Jefferson Looney. Princeton: Princeton University Press, 2013, pp. 654–655.]

[11] "To Thomas Jefferson from Maria Cosway, [1 December? 1787]," *Founders Online*, National Archives, https://founders.archives.gov/documents/Jefferson/01-12-02-0390. [Original source: *The Papers of Thomas Jefferson*, vol. 12, *7 August 1787–31 March 1788*, ed. Julian P. Boyd. Princeton: Princeton University Press, 1955, p. 387.]

Cosway is surprised, even flattered, by the event in her honor. Moreover, there is Cosway's mysterious line, "If my inclination had been your law, I should have had the pleasure of seeing you More then I have." There are two ways of cashing out the claim, made ambiguous by Cosway's lack of facility with English. First, the law to which Cosway refers might be Jefferson's wish that she should spend all her free time with him. If so, then to grasp the counterfactual nature of the claim, we must take her "inclination" not to be Jefferson's "law." The sentence implies displeasure with Jefferson. Cosway is eschewing Jefferson's company. A more charitable and reasonable interpretation is to understand Jefferson's law by her inclination—her wish to have seen Jefferson much more than she has seen him. That agrees with her feeling unpleasantly "the *loss*," yet there is no mention of the loss being profound, and she turns forthwith to her disbelief, once back in London, that her time in Paris has come to an end. Nonetheless, there is little in this brief communication that shows any strong feelings for Jefferson.

What happens at the send-off party?

That question Jefferson answers in an early letter to Cosway in 1788.

On the day of her departure (December 8), Jefferson plans on breakfasting with Cosway—she has agreed to do so—and perhaps traveling with her once again to Saint-Denis. Yet Cosway leaves on an earlier coach. The *coup de grace* is a breviloquent letter she leaves behind for Jefferson.

### "I leave you with very melancholy ideas"

## MC to TJ, London, 7 Dec. 1787

I cannot breakfast with you to morrow; to bid you adieu once is sufficiently painful, for I leave you with very melancholy ideas. You have given my dear Sir all your commissions to Mr. Trumbull, and I have the reflection that I cannot be useful to you; who have rendered me so many civilities.[12]

Cosway's letter of *adieu* is no *au revoir*. Something has happened between the two and Cosway wants to have little, or nothing, to do with Jefferson—at least not *tête-à-tête*. Do the two meet just after Cosway arrives in Paris in 1787 and does Jefferson again come on too strong? As I show in *Thomas Jefferson:*

---

[12] "To Thomas Jefferson from Maria Cosway, [7 December 1787]," *Founders Online*, National Archives, https://founders.archives.gov/documents/Jefferson/01-12-02-0412. [Original source: *The Papers of Thomas Jefferson*, vol. 12, *7 August 1787-31 March 1788*, ed. Julian P. Boyd. Princeton: Princeton University Press, 1955, p. 403.]

*Psychobiography of an American Lion,* Jefferson is maladroit with women.[13] One has merely to consider how he botches his early-in-life relationship with Rebecca Burwell, and his effusive, but somewhat ham-handed *billet doux* to Cosway and Cosway's inability to respond, because she is overwhelmed.

When Cosway is in London, she offers Jefferson a fuller explanation for her failure to appear for breakfast.

### "I was Confus'd and distracted"
## MC to TJ, London, 10 Dec. 1787

My dear friend

You promised to come to breakfast with Me the Morning of My departure, and to Accompany me part of the way, did you go? I left Paris with Much regret indeed, I could not bear to take leave any More. I was Confus'd and distracted, you Must have thought me so when you saw me in the Evening; why is it My fortune to find Amiable people where I go, and why am I to be obliged to part with them! T'is very Cruel: I hope our Correspondance will be More frequent and punctual then our Meetings were while I was in Paris. I suspected the reason, and would not reproach you since I know your Objection to Company. You are happy you can follow so Much your inclinations. I wish I could do the same. I do all I can, but with little success, perhaps I dont know how to go about it.

We have had a very good journey, except the two last days I was very ill. It has been a pleasure to Me to find My relations and friends, but it does not lessen the pain of finding My self so far from those of Paris. Accept this short letter this time. I Mean to send a Much longer one soon, but Mean while answer Me this by a long one. I hope your lovely daughters are well. Remember Me to Mr. Short, & believe me ever Yours Most affly.,

M. Cosway[14]

Cosway again says very little that might heal Jefferson's wounds. Confused and distracted, she regrets leaving Paris, but she says nothing about any pain in parting from Jefferson. Her pain, she says, is in finding amiable people

---

[13] M. Andrew Holowchak, *Thomas Jefferson: Psychobiography of an American Lion* (Hauppague, NY: Nova, 2019), chap. 2.

[14] "To Thomas Jefferson from Maria Cosway, 10 December [1787]," *Founders Online*, National Archives, https://founders.archives.gov/documents/Jefferson/01-12-02-0421. [Original source: *The Papers of Thomas Jefferson*, vol. 12, *7 August 1787-31 March 1788*, ed. Julian P. Boyd. Princeton: Princeton University Press, 1955, p. 415.]

wherever she travels and then having to part with them. Jefferson is, again, just one such amiable person.

The last letter of 1787 is sent by Cosway to Jefferson on Christmas Day.

### "And what did you think of me?"
## MC to TJ, London, 25 Dec. 1787

How do you do My dear friend? You came to the invitation of my breakfast the Morning of my departure! and what did you think of Me? I did it to avoid the last taking leave, I went too early for any body to see Me. I cannot express how Miserable I was in leaving Paris. How I regreted not having seen More of you, and I cannot have even the Satisfaction to unburden My displeasure of [it] by loading you with reproches. Your reasons Must be Sufficient, and My forcing you would have [been] unkind and unfriendly as it woud be cruel to pretend on what is totaly disagreable to you. Another reason keeps ever since I am perfectly sure t'was My fault but my Misfortune, and then we can bear to be Contradicted in our wishes with More resignation.

Have you seen yet the lovely Mrs. Church? You Must have seen her by this time: what do you think of her? She Colls' me her Sister. I coll' her My dearest Sister. If I did not love her so Much I should fear her rivalship, but no I give you free permission to love her with all your heart, and I shall feel happy if I think you keep me in a little corner of it, when you admit her even to reing [reign]Queen.

I have not receivd any letter from you. I feel the loss of it. Make it up by sending Me very long ones and tell Me all you do how you pass your time. When you are at your Hermitage, all that regards you will be interesting to me. Have you seen Any of the.... Gentlemen who I had the honor to introduce to you and who received so politly. The Abbè Piatolli is a wor[thy Man?] Mr. Niemicewiz a very Amiable gen[tleman...] the Prince Charteressi worthy of [...] Manners Custums and principles you [embrace?] improve him in all he has so far [on account of?] Natural disposition and talent!

Again I request write to Me [....]

My best Compliments to Mr. Short and believe dear sir Yours Most Affly,

Maria Cosway[15]

---

[15] "To Thomas Jefferson from Maria Cosway, 25 December [1787]," *Founders Online*, National Archives, https://founders.archives.gov/documents/Jefferson/01-12-02-0469. [Original source: *The Papers of Thomas Jefferson*, vol. 12, *7 August 1787-31 March 1788*, ed. Julian P. Boyd. Princeton: Princeton University Press, 1955, pp. 459–460.]

Cosway, now at a comfortable distance from Jefferson, can resume her coquettish ways. She explains that she had left Paris early because of the pain of leaving Paris and her regret of not having seen more of Jefferson. So pained is she that she has not even the energy to burden Jefferson with reproaches.

It is singular to note that Jefferson has penned only one letter this year to Cosway—a sure sign of some recognition that there is now a wedge between them—that can be nothing romantic between them.

Chapter III

# The Year 1788

Early in the spring of 1788, Jefferson travels directly to the Netherlands to meet with John Adams in an effort to consolidate and extend American loans secured through Dutch brokers in some effort for the young country to pay its debts.[1] On his return to Paris, he takes an anfractuous route, as he tours the Netherlands and German Rhineland *en route* back to Paris. The trip overall will take him seven weeks, and along the way, he will often think of Cosway, though he will not find a suitable occasion to pen to her a letter.[2]

Yet prior to leaving for the long trip, Jefferson writes a letter to Cosway to express his dismay upon her early departure for London on December 8, 1787, and her failure to meet him for the planned early breakfast.

There are 11 letters exchanged this year: five by Cosway, six by Jefferson.

### "En petite comitté"
### TJ to MC, Paris, 31 Jan. 1788

I went to breakfast with you according to promise, and you had gone off at 5. oclock in the morning. This spared me indeed the pain of parting, but it deprives me of the comfort of recollecting that pain. Your departure was the signal of distress to your friends.

You know the accident which so long confined the Princess to her room. Madame de Corny too was immediately thrown into great alarm for the life of her husband. After being long at death's door he is reviving. Mrs. Church seemed to come to participate of the distress of her friend instead of the pleasures of Paris. I never saw her before: but I find in her all the good the world has given her credit for. I do not wonder at your fondness for each other. I have seen too little of her, as I did of you.

But in your case it was not my fault, unless it be a fault to love my friends so dearly as to wish to enjoy their company in the only way it yeilds enjoiment,

---

[1] For more, see George Green Shackelford, *Thomas Jefferson's Travels in Europe, 1784–1789* (Baltimore: Johns Hopkins University Press, 1995), 129–31.
[2] Thomas Jefferson, "Memorandum Books, 1788," *Founders Online*, National Archives, https://founders.archives.gov/documents/Jefferson/02-0I-02-0022, accessed 13 Aug. 2021.

that is, en petite comité.³ You make every body love you. You are sought and surrounded therefore by all. Your mere domestic cortege was so numerous, et si imposante, that one could not approach you quite at their ease. Nor could you so unpremeditately mount into the Phaeton and hide away to the bois de Boulogne, St. Cloud, Marly, St. Germains &c. Add to this the distance at which you were placed from me. When you come again, you must be nearer, and move more extempore.

You complain, my dear Madam, of my not writing to you, and you have the appearance of cause for complaint. But I have been above a month looking out for a private conveiance, without being able to find one, and you know the infidelity of the post office. Sometimes they mislay letters to pocket the frankmoney: and always they open those of people in office. As if your friendship and mine could be interesting to government! As if, instead of the effusions of a sincere esteem, we would fill our letters with the miserable trash called state secrets!

I am flattered by your attention to me in the affair of the tea vase. I like perfectly the form of the one Mrs. Church brought. But Mr. Trumbull and myself have seen one made for the count de Moustier, wherein the spout is suppressed, and the water made to issue at a pretty little ornament. When he returns he will explain this to you, and try to get me a vase of the size and form of Mrs. Church's, but with this improvement. In this business I shall beg leave to associate your taste with his.

Present my compliments to Mr. Cosway. I am obliged to trust this letter through the post office, as I see no immediate chance of a private conveiance.

Adieu, my dear Madam: think of me often and warmly, as I do of you.⁴

The letter is the only evidence, and certainly not direct, of what happens at Cosway's *bon voyage* party. Jefferson speaks of Cosway's "domestic cortege," and that is clearly a reference to the group of persons that ever seem to be around Cosway at her residence and very likely at the party at Hôtel de Langeac.

Biographers and scholars go to great lengths to salvage the notion that Cosway loved Jefferson. I proffer two instances. Gerald Barnett maintains that Cosway distances herself from Jefferson at least in part because of intimate

---

³ In small company.
⁴ "From Thomas Jefferson to Maria Cosway, [31] January [1788]," *Founders Online*, National Archives, https://founders.archives.gov/documents/Jefferson/01-12-02-0576. [Original source: *The Papers of Thomas Jefferson*, vol. 12, *7 August 1787-31 March 1788*, ed. Julian P. Boyd. Princeton: Princeton University Press, 1955, pp. 539–540.]

involvement with "so many hardened [Polish] veterans of war and power politics" through her involvement with Princess Lubomirski and the nodi concerning Polish statehood at the time, evidenced by Cosway's letters.[5] John Kaminski states that both are stubborn. Each waits for the other to make an effusive, open expression of love. Cosway, it seems, is willing to express her love but waits for Jefferson first to do so.[6] That fails to accommodate Jefferson's unequivocal but clumsy expression of love on October 12, 1786. Cosway has had ample time to reply likewise and has not, and that explains Jefferson's increasing coolth—he has been battered by Cosway since his *billet doux*—in subsequent letters.

Yet Jefferson's use of "cortege" suggests flatterers—that is, suitors other than Jefferson. If Jefferson has something significant to tell Cosway on that evening, does he get the chance to articulate it? Having intentionally spent her months in Paris away from Jefferson, it is almost certain that she has instructed friends at the party never to leave her alone with Jefferson. I iterate: When people want to be together, they find ways to be together. Cosway fails to show up for breakfast prior to her departure for London in December 1787 because she anticipates Jefferson's full expression of love, which she wishes to eschew.

### "My war against you"
## MC to TJ, London, 6 Mar. 1788

I have waited some time to trie [try] if I could recover my usual peace with you, but I find it is impossible yet, therefore Must adress Myself to you still *angry*. Your long silence is impardonable, but what is the Name I Must give To ***** Mr: Trumbull and Mrs: Church not bringing Me a letter from you? No, My war against you is of such a Nature that I cannot even find terms to express it. Yet I will not be in your debt. I think it a great One since it is to acknowledge *one* letter from you, *One* and *short*, however I beleave that realy you know how I value every line which comes from you, why will you add scarcity? But I begin to runn on and my intention was only to say, *nothing*, send a blank paper; as a Lady in a Passion is not fit for Any thing. What shall you do when you will be Much farther, I can't bare the idea.

---

[5] Gerald Barnett, *Richard and Maria Cosway: A Biography* (Cambridge: The Lutterworth Press, 1995), 103–4.
[6] John Kaminski, *Jefferson in Love: The Love Letters beteen Thomas Jefferson & Maria Cosway* (Lanham, MD: 1999), 20.

Will you give Mr: Trumbull leave to Make a Coppy of a certain portrait he painted at Paris? It is a person who hates you that requests this favor. If you want private conveiance to send me a letter there are many. Ask Abbe Piattoli, Madme: de Corney, and Many others. Tho' I am angry I can hardly end My letter. Remember, I do you justice by not thinking of you now.[7]

This is another scolding letter from Cosway—the most ireful scolding letter that she has hitherto written. Angry and fraught with hatred, says she, Cosway is a lady in passion who is at war with Jefferson, and the letter is unsigned—that certainly done with intention.

It is here important to pause and, as it were, to take inventory. Why is a person who makes every effort to avoid Jefferson in Paris so consumed by irefulness? What are Jefferson's thoughts on the reception of this livid letter?

Cosway has no love for Jefferson, at least not in the manner in which Jefferson loves Cosway, nonetheless, she remains, in her own words, an *enfant gatée*. As I say in Chapter 1, she knows that she has hooked Jefferson, and she is not wont to let anyone, once hooked, get unhooked—especially a significant American dignitary and a man of lofty notions and with significant global connections.

In contrast, Jefferson's head, having lost a significant battle with his heart in the *billet doux* of October 1786, has, at this point, won the war. Although he undoubtedly still has feelings for Cosway, they have much attenuated, and she no longer occupies a significant place in his thoughts. Does Jefferson find the game Cosway is playing an annoyance or amusing, or has he merely become, at this point, stolid? Not being a person who is readily annoyed, it is probable that Jefferson's attitude shifts between amusement—I cannot but think that he has a laugh when he reads of her hatred of him—and stolidity. Some degree of stolidity has certainly set in on account of her constant rebuffs. Yet he continues the correspondence, though his letters will be less frequent, less long, and less effusive, and continuance is evidence that he at least finds Cosway's paroxysms somewhat entertaining—part of the charm of the woman. He certainly, at this point, sees through the charade.

When Jefferson returns to his residence in Paris from his trip to the Netherlands, he finds a "bushel of letters." He unquestionably sorts them in terms of their importance. Among the important letters, he finds one from Cosway, and he opens it before all others. That Jefferson sifts through his pile of

---

[7] "To Thomas Jefferson from Maria Cosway, 6 March 1788," *Founders Online*, National Archives, https://founders.archives.gov/documents/Jefferson/01-12-02-0705. [Original source: *The Papers of Thomas Jefferson*, vol. 12, *7 August 1787-31 March 1788*, ed. Julian P. Boyd. Princeton: Princeton University Press, 1955, p. 645.]

letters and looks for one from Cosway is a sure sign that he is still in some measure under her spell.

### "I am but a son of nature"
## TJ to MC, Paris, 24 Apr. 1788

I arrived here, my dear friend, the last night, and in a bushel of letters presented me by way of reception, I saw that one was of your handwriting. It is the only one I have yet opened, and I answer it before I open another. I do not think I was in arrears in our epistolary account when I left Paris. In affection I am sure you were greatly my debtor.

I often determined during my journey to write to you: but sometimes the fatigue of exercise, and sometimes a fatigued attention hindered me. At Dusseldorp I wished for you much. I surely never saw so precious a collection of paintings. Above all things those of Van der Werff affected me the most. His picture of Sarah delivering Agar to Abraham is delicious. I would have agreed to have been Abraham though the consequence would have been that I should have been dead five or six thousand years. Carlo Dolce became also a violent favorite. I am so little of a connoisseur that I preferred the works of these two authors to the old faded red things of Rubens. I am but a son of nature, loving what I see and feel, without being able to give a reason, nor caring much whether there be one. At Heidelberg I wished for you too. In fact I led you by the hand thro' the whole garden. I was struck with the resemblance of this scene to that of Vaucluse as seen from what is called the chateau of Petrarch. Nature has formed both on the same sketch, but she has filled up that of Heidelberg with a bolder hand. The river is larger, the mountains more majestic and better clothed. Art too has seconded her views. The chateau of Petrarch is the ruin of a modest country house, that of Heidelbourg would stand well along side the pyramids of Egypt. It is certainly the most magnificent ruin after those left us by the antients. At Strasbourg I sat down to write to you. But for my soul I could think of nothing at Strasbourg but the promontory of noses, of Diego, of Slawkenburgius his historian, and the procession of the Strasburgers to meet the man with the nose. Had I written to you from thence it would have been a continuation of Sterne upon noses, and I knew that nature had not formed me for a Continuator of Sterne: so I let it alone till I came here and received your angry letter. It is a proof of your esteem, but I love better to have soft testimonials of it. You must therefore now write me a letter teeming with affection; such as I feel for you. So much I have no right to ask.

Being but just arrived I am not au fait of the small news respecting your acquaintance here. I know only that the princess Lubomirski is still here, and that she has taken the house that was M. de Simoulin's. When you come again therefore you will be somewhat nearer to me, but not near enough: and still surrounded by a numerous cortege, so that I shall see you only by scraps as I did when you were here last. The time before we were half days, and whole days together, and I found this too little. Adieu! God bless you! Your's affectionately,

Th: Jefferson[8]

 

    The letter is one of the most charming of the correspondence. While *en route* back to Paris—at Dusseldorp, at Heidelberg, and at Strasbourg—Jefferson often thinks of Cosway, when he views the galleries that he tours or the bold and sublime scenes created by man or by nature—e.g., the Castle of Heidelberg, nestled in a rocky hill, filled with saxicolous trees. Yet he admits that the lure to write Cosway is overwhelmed by physical or attentional fatigue, and that is a sentiment that is intended to sting Cosway. She has often hurt him, and it is time for her to feel some of the hurt that he has often felt.

    Jefferson's letter has its intended effect. Cosway writes five days later, certainly on the day of her reception of Jefferson's missive, and Cosway is once again ireful. Cosway feels the sting of indifference.

### "Not to find one word to write, *but on Noses*"
## MC to TJ, London, 29 Apr. 1788

At last I receive a letter from you, am I to be angry or not? I think when we go to question and doubt it is a good syng [thing?], tho' I dont know whether it is in favor of you or the Manner in which you appollogies. Many Contradictions will make me answer article by article your letter; My hand for writing made you Open my letter in preferance to all the others you received on your arrival, I am not obliged *to you* for this distinction. Sympathy, and remorse have my acknoledgements.

    Afterwards lett me tell you I am not your debtor in the least. The fatigue of your journey the different occupations the & & & & prevented your writing, I agree, but how could you led me by the hand all the way, think of me, have Many things to say, and not find One word to write, *but on Noses?* No, this I cannot put up with, it is too bad, and what is worse it is not indolence, it is what I must add to my Misfortunes, and I never thought your name was to be on *that* list.

---

[8] "To Thomas Jefferson from Maria Cosway, 6 March 1788," *Founders Online,* National Archives, https://founders.archives.gov/documents/Jefferson/01-12-02-0705. [Original source: *The Papers of Thomas Jefferson,* vol. 12, *7 August 1787–31 March 1788,* ed. Julian P. Boyd. Princeton: Princeton University Press, 1955, p. 645.]

You say my letter was angry, You acknowledge it is a proof of esteem, but you prefer softer testimonies of it. Give me the example if you please. Am I to adress a stranger in such confidential terms? who writs to me so short and scarse as possible?

Oh I wish My dear friend I could announce to you our return to Paris! I am afraid to question My Lord and Master on this subject; he may not think or like to refuse, and a disappointed promise of this kind would be too cruel to me. I cannot bear it. I should be doubly Miserable all the Summer; but why dont you Come? Your friend Mr: de la Luzerne is here, Mrs. Church, we should go to see Many beautifull villas, enjoy all the best England can afford and make the rest up with our own Society; we shall not have a Numerous Cortege, I promise to Make Myself and my Society according to your own wish. At home we may do it better, if I come to Paris I may do more what I please this time. There are but four people I could wish to pass all my time with. Is this too great a Number? when *you* are One, even if you dont guess the others I am Sure you would not object to. I long to return. I left a bad impression in the atmosphier. I was worse then myself, and realy so bad that Sometimes I hardly knew Myself. I am Much better now, and My Constant occupations for these three Months past keep me in better health or they keep me in better spirits, and that is the Most dangerous Malady I can have.

If you want to hear what Italian Singing is, come to London. Marchesi is here and the Most wonderfull Singer I ever heard. The Opera is good but for want of equal performers with him it is rather dull as the whole spectacle depending on one person, makes the rest appear tiresome. We shall have a New One very soon and wonders are expected.

I cannot announce the portrait of a friend of mine in my Study yet, Trumbull puts me out of all patiance. I allways thought painting slow work, 'tis dreadfull now.

How is Mr: Short? Pray remember me to him in the kindest Manner, the beauty he lost his heart by is here keeling every body with her beweching Eyes.

Say many things to Madme: de Corney. I love her very Much and I will add that word to her Husband too. When you see any body I know speak of me if they are agreable t'will improve the subject, if they love me I shall be recalld to your remembrance with partiality. I would wish to deserve and nourish the good Opinion you have of me from your own Sentiments, inforce it by those you esteem, and oblige you from a return of the affection & friendship I feel for you to allow without bounds you will allways be deficient to

Maria Cosway

Mr. Cosway presents his Compliments.⁹

Cosway must be irate. Jefferson, she notes, often thinks of her and leads her by the hand through his excursions, but he has not the energy to write to her. Her inclusion of "& & & &" shows that she believes Jefferson is of the disposition to think of any excuse not to write. She recognizes that Jefferson aims to hurt her, and she acknowledges that he has succeeded. Cosway singles out Jefferson's reference to "noses" at Strasbourg as a singular insult, but she fails nevertheless to recognize that it is one of all too few illustrations of Jefferson's dry and inaccessible humor.¹⁰

Cosway then turns to Jefferson's question of her return to Paris the next year. She can make no promise, but she enjoins Jefferson to come to London. She promises not to have a large cortege, though there still will be a cortege. Cosway stings back at Jefferson. He is but one of four people with whom Cosway might wish to spend all her time. "Is this too great a Number? when *you* are one."

There is also mention in the letter a trip to the opera where Cosway has the pleasure of hearing the world's most celebrated singer, castrato Gaetano Luigi Marchesi, who has come to London in the spring. Of his performance, critic Mount-Edgcumbe says: "His acting was spirited and expressive; his vocal powers were very great, his voice of extensive compass, but a little inclined to be thick. His execution was very considerable, and he was rather too fond of displaying it, nor was his cantabile singing equal to his bravura."¹¹ She probably sends Marchesi an invitation to her residence at Schomberg House to perform in person during the Monday night musical sessions, and he is soon a regular at the mansion on Mondays. The two form a fast friendship. On July 2, London's *Morning Post* publishes a scandalous piece on their unusual relationship.

> The charms of the fair Maria Cosway were so alluring in the eyes of Marchesi on Saturday last at the opera, that between the acts of *Guilo Sabino* he went into the same box with the seductive artist & remained

---

⁹ "To Thomas Jefferson from Maria Cosway, 29 April 1788," *Founders Online*, National Archives, https://founders.archives.gov/documents/Jefferson/01-13-02-0042. [Original source: *The Papers of Thomas Jefferson*, vol. 13, *March–7 October 1788*, ed. Julian P. Boyd. Princeton: Princeton University Press, 1956, pp. 114–116.]

¹⁰ The aside is a reference to Sterne's lengthy, playful digression concerning the length of noses, beginning at vol. 3, chap. 31, in *Tristram Shandy, Gentleman*. The stranger's large nose likely symbolizes his distended penis in recognition of a lost lover, and that is likely.

¹¹ Helen Duprey Bullock, *My Head and My Heart: A Little History of Thomas Jefferson and Maria Cosway* (New York: G.P. Putnam's Sons, 1945), 49.

there in tender homage till his theatrical duties called him again to the stage. The lady sat in the box next to the stage, so that this trip of the warbling hero being in full in sight of the audience could not be deemed in the highest degree respectful.[12]

Cosway's relationship with Marchesi is discussed more fully in Chapter 4.

Jefferson does not reply, and Cosway pens another scolding letter—this one curt.

### "I will write two words…"
## MC to TJ, London, 23 June 1788

I will write two words, to show you I can write *if I please* but as I dont please I shall say no More, as I wait to hear from you. If my silence is of consequence, you will easily be sensible that yours is Very much so with me, but [I] must have patience, oh I break my first intention.

So addio M. Cosway

Should I have wrote so much if Mr. Trumbull had not Come to ask me to send a letter by a person who is going to see you? Ask yourself if you deserve it? Or if it is not only a spontanous inclination, or irrestibility to this temptation, tho' you neglect me, I force myself to your recolection.[13]

In the next few weeks, there is still no letter from Jefferson, so Cosway drafts another letter, much softer in tone, to lure a reply.

### "What does your silence Mean, My dear friend!"
## MC to TJ, London, 15 July 1788

Is it possible that I write another letter before I have My answer from My two last! What can be the reason? It is either obstinacy, or Constancy in Me: but what does your silence Mean My dear friend! It seems that opportunities supposedly force themselves on you to recal me to your remembrances, should I have

---

[12] Carol Burnell, *Divided Affections: The Extraordinary Life of Maria Cosway: Celebrity Artist and Thomas Jefferson's Impossible Love* (London: Column House, 2007), 242.

[13] "To Thomas Jefferson from Maria Cosway, 23 June 1788," *Founders Online,* National Archives, https://founders.archives.gov/documents/Jefferson/01-13-02-0187. [Original source: *The Papers of Thomas Jefferson*, vol. 13, *March–7 October 1788*, ed. Julian P. Boyd. Princeton: Princeton University Press, 1956, pp. 287–288.]

otherwise so much Courage or should I be so bold as to *insist* in a corrispondance! Mr: St: André is Coming to Paris and ask's me particularly for a letter to you, when I think of you I forgit all formality I only remember your kindness, your friendship. You cannot change; it is only by chance (and that is seldom) if I think of you that I suppose I could not write to any body that does not think of me; then a string of *punctellios* and *formalités* stand frowning before me waiting for the happy time, which brings me letters to answer. Such is the situation of your Most affte:

Maria Cosway in waiting[14]


Cosway's letter has its intended effect. In a couple of weeks, Jefferson crafts a reply.

### "The Maria who makes Hours her own"
## TJ to MC, Paris, 27 July 1788

Hail, dear friend of mine! For I am never so happy as when business, smoothing her magisterial brow, says 'I give you an hour to converse with your friends.' And with none do I converse more fondly than with my good Maria: not her under the poplar, with the dog and string at her girdle: but the Maria who makes the Hours her own, who teaches them to dance for us in so charming a round, and lets us think of nothing but her who renders them *si gracieuses.* Your Hours [Figure 3-1],[15] my dear friend, are no longer your own. Every body now demands them; and were it possible for me to want a memorandum of you, it is presented me in every street of Paris. Come then to see what triumph Time is giving you. Come and see every body stopping to admire the Hours, suspended against the walls of the Quai des Augustins, the Boulevards, the Palais royal &c. &c. with a 'Maria Cosway delint' at the bottom.

---

[14] "To Thomas Jefferson from Maria Cosway, 15 July 1788," *Founders Online,* National Archives, https://founders.archives.gov/documents/Jefferson/01-13-02-0264. [Original source: *The Papers of Thomas Jefferson,* vol. 13, *March–7 October 1788,* ed. Julian P. Boyd. Princeton: Princeton University Press, 1956, pp. 360–361.]

[15] Cosway's recent painting *The Hours.* For more, see Luisa Calè, "Maria Cosway's *Hours:* Cosmopolitan and Classical Visual Culture in Thoma Makin's Poets Gallery, *Romanticism and Illustration,* ed. Ian Haywood, Susan Matthews, and Mary L. Shannon (Cambridge University Press, 2019), 221–42.

**Figure 3-1:** Francesco Bartolozzi, *Engraving of Cosway's painting*, 1788

Source: Wikipedia

But you triumph every where; so, if you come here, it will be, not to see your triumphs but your friends, and to make them happy with your presence. Indeed we wish much for you. Society here is become more gloomy than usual. The civil dissensions, tho' they have yet cost no blood and will I hope cost none, still render conversation serious, and society contentious. How gladly would I take refuge every day in your coterie. Your benevolence, embracing all parties, disarms the party-dispositions of your friends, and makes of yours an asylum for tranquility. We are told you are becoming more recluse. This is a proof the more of your taste. A great deal of love given to a few, is better than a little to many. Besides, the world will derive greater benefit from your talents, as these will be less called off from their objects by numerous visits. I remember that when under the hands of your Coëffeuse, you used to amuse yourself with your pencil. Take then, some of these days, when Fancy bites and the Coeffeuse is busy, a little visiting card, and crayon on it something for me. What shall it be? Cupid leading the lion by a thread? Or Minerva clipping his wings? Or shall it be political? The father, for instance, giving the bunch of rods to his children to break, or Jupiter sending to the frogs a kite instead of the log for their king? Or shall it be something better than all this, a sketch of your own fancy? So that I have something from your hand, it will satisfy me; and it will be the better if of your own imagination. I will put a 'Maria Cosway delint.'[16] At bottom, and stamp it on my visiting cards, that our names may be

---

[16] "Painted by Maria Cosway."

together if our persons cannot. Adieu, my dear friend, love me much, and love me always. Your's affectionately,

Th: Jefferson[17]

Jefferson proffers a warm and affable reply to Cosway's soft scolding letter. He refers throughout and approvingly to Cosway's painting, *The Hours*, which has recently gone to print with a beautiful engraving by Francesco Bartolozzi. The painting itself is ambiguously received by critics. Peter Pindar unsurprisingly mocks Cosways' choice of coloration and exaggeration of figures:

> No, No! with all my lyric powers
> I'm not like Mrs. Cosway's Hours,
> Red as cock-turkies, plump as barn-door chicken.
> Merit and I are miserably off;
> We both have got a most consumptive cough,
> Hunger hath long our harmless bones been picking.[18]

Bartolozzi's prints make the painting popular.

Jefferson adds that he will be honored if Cosway makes for him a little sketch of her choosing with crayon or pencil for him to have and cherish. There is here no sense of longing for Cosway but merely pride in her aesthetic achievement. There is also recognition that there can be no romantic relationship between the two, as Jefferson, with delight, consents to be among the few in her "coterie." He adds, "Your benevolence, embracing all parties, disarms the party-dispositions of your friends, and makes of yours an asylum for tranquility." The implication here is that some or all in her coterie of close friends are crass and have underhanded motives in aiming to be near her. Yet Cosway's goodness disarms the deceit. Jefferson here is emotionally drawing from Cosway.

Three days later, Jefferson drafts another letter to Cosway—ostensibly to prevent another scolding letter because he cannot often write to her. Yet the emotion returns to his quill, as this letter betrays large vulnerability. It is perhaps evidence that he regrets the emotionless letter of three days ago.

---

[17] "From Thomas Jefferson to Maria Cosway, 27 July 1788," *Founders Online*, National Archives, https://founders.archives.gov/documents/Jefferson/01-13-02-0311. [Original source: *The Papers of Thomas Jefferson*, vol. 13, *March–7 October 1788*, ed. Julian P. Boyd. Princeton: Princeton University Press, 1956, pp. 423–424.]

[18] Peter Pindar, Ode I, *More Lyric Odes, to the Roayl Academicians* (London: 1783).

### "Chide me then no more"
### TJ to MC, Paris, 30 July 1788

My dear dear friend

Cease to chide me. It is hard to have been chained to a writing table, drudging over business daily from morning to night ever since my return to Paris. It will be a cruel exaggeration, if I am to lose my friends into the bargain. The only letter of private friendship I wrote on my return, and before entering on business, was to you. The first I wrote after getting through my budget was to you. It had gone off on the morning of the last post, and in the evening of the same day, your's of the 15th. was brought here by I know not whom, while I was out.

I am incapable of forgetting or neglecting you my dear friend; and I am sure if the comparison could be fairly made of how much I think of you, or you of me, the former scale would greatly preponderate. Of this I have no right to complain, nor do I complain. You esteem me as much as I deserve. If I love you more, it is because you deserve more. Of voluntary faults to you I can never be guilty, and you are too good not to pardon the involuntary. Chide me then no more; be to me what you have been; and give me without measure the comfort of your friendship. *Adieu ma tres chere et excellente amie.*

Th: J.[19]


Beginning with "My dear dear friend," Cosway is on Jefferson's mawkish mind. He thinks of her much more than she thinks of him, but that is how it must be. Her lack of esteem for him is due to desert. She loves him in proportion to his worth; he, to her worth. Denial and depression have morphed into acceptance of what is the case. "Be to me what you have been," he writes, and implicitly, "not what I want you to be." Jefferson here is fully broken. He has come to realize that he does not deserve to be loved by her.

### "Next to the pleasure of seeing one's friends…"
### MC to TJ, Down Place, 19 Aug. 1788

Many thanks My dear friend for your two letters, had I not reason to scold you? was such a long Silence friendly? and can you wish me not to take notice of it?

---

[19] "From Thomas Jefferson to Maria Cosway, 30 July 1788," *Founders Online*, National Archives, https://founders.archives.gov/documents/Jefferson/01-13-02-0328. [Original source: *The Papers of Thomas Jefferson*, vol. 13, *March–7 October 1788*, ed. Julian P. Boyd. Princeton: Princeton University Press, 1956, p. 435.]

No, that would be a Mark of too great an indiferance; Next to the pleasure of seing ones friends, is that of hearing from them; I never think so much of the distance we are from them, as the lenght of time we dont hear from them.

I am Much flatterd by what you say of My Hours. I am happy you like the Idea, and the Author of that subject has every gratification and recompence by the wish she has inspired you with, of possessing some of her work.

I thank you for giving me an opportunity of sending you a little souvenir of a talent that she would wish to possess in a higher degree that the Picture might be More deserving of being hung up in the room you inhabit Most that she may be recald to your remembrance as often as possible. I shall endevor to find a subject suited to your taste, you describe several, and all good, I shall see what I can do from your painting out your choice. I am at present in the Country therefore it is impossible to begin immediatly an occupation I shall feel most happy when engaged about it, as I have nothing with me to paint with, nor any convineance for it.

Where do you think I am at present? and with whom? How Much we wish for you and think of you and speak of you, it is the amiable Mrs: Church, you know her, that is enough, and you are Capable of feeling the value of this lovely woman.

I have been Made very uneasy with the news that you intend to return soon to America, is it true? and is it possible! Oh then I give up the hopes of ever seing you again; wont' you come to pay us a visit first, it is but a little jurney for so Much pleasure you will procure us, pray lett me intreat you to Make me this promise. But we have hopes of going to Italy soon, I am doing every thing I can, use every argument, to make Mr: Cosway go next year, then My dear friend you should be of the party can you resist this proposition! I leave you to consider of it, and write to Me very soon. Mr: Cosway desires his best Compliments, and Mrs. Church has told me to say many things to you; I reccomand My self to be admitted to half she deserves of affection from you, t'will be a good share but never so much as I have for you—adiu.

Wish me joy for I possess your Picture. Trumbull has procured me the happiness which I shall ever be gratfull for.[20]

Cosway again scolds, but mildly, gently. She must be astonished to have received two letters from Jefferson in four days. In response to his letter of July

---

[20] "To Thomas Jefferson from Maria Cosway, 19 August 1788," *Founders Online*, National Archives, https://founders.archives.gov/documents/Jefferson/01-13-02-0404. [Original source: *The Papers of Thomas Jefferson*, vol. 13, *March–7 October 1788*, ed. Julian P. Boyd. Princeton: Princeton University Press, 1956, pp. 524–525.]

27, she consents to do a little painting for Jefferson suited to his taste so "that she may be recald to your remembrance as often as possible." She adds that she has heard rumor of Jefferson's return to the New World and dreads the news, or so she says.

Jefferson replies to Cosway's letter some two months after his last letter. He requests that Cosway merely send to him on a visiting card merely a few strokes of her pencil, for he wishes not to trespass on her time.

Jefferson laments that as she travels to Italy and he to America, the two will be even father parted, and that cannot be good. He instructs her on what to see in Italy but quickly disadvises such a trip and advises instead a trip to America with Angela Church. The natural mirabilia of the United States have not been studied and copied much by talented artists. Those of Italy have.

### "But why go to Italy?"

## TJ to MC, Paris, 26 Sept. 1788

Your favor of Aug. the 19., my very dear friend, is put into my hands this 26th. day of September 1788. and I answer it in the same instant to shew you there is nothing nearer my heart than to meet all the testimonies of your esteem. It is a strong one that you will occupy yourself for me on such a trifle as a visiting card. But sketch it only with your pencil, my friend, and do not make of it a serious business. This would render me uneasy, because I did not mean such a trespass on your time. A few strokes of your pencil on a card will be enjoiment enough for me.

I am going to America, and you to Italy. The one or the other of us goes the wrong way, for the way will ever be wrong which leads us farther apart. Mine is a journey of duty and of affection. I must deposit my daughters in the bosom of their friends and country. This done, I shall return to my station. My absence may be as short as five months, and certainly not longer than nine. How long my subsequent stay here may be I cannot tell. It would certainly be the longer had I a single friend here like yourself.

In going to Italy, be sure to cross the Alps at the Col de Tende. It is the best pass, because you need never get out of your carriage. It is practicable in seasons when all the other passes are shut up by snow. The roads leading to and from it are as fine as can possibly be, and you will see the castle of Saorgio. Take a good day for that part of your journey, and when you shall have sketched it in your portefeuille, and copied it more at leisure for yourself, tear out the leaf and send it to me.

But why go to Italy? You have seen it, all the world has seen it, and ransacked it thousands of times. Rather join our good friend Mrs. Church in her trip to

America. There you will find original scenes, scenes worthy of your pencil, such as the Natural bridge or the Falls of Niagara. Or participate with Trumbull the historical events of that country. These will have the double merit of being new, and of coming from you. I should find excuses for being sometimes of your parties. Think of this, my dear friend, mature the project with Mrs. Church, and let us all embark together at Havre. Adieu ma tres chere et excellente amie. Your's affectionately,

Th: J.[21]

The final letter of the year is penned by Cosway.

### "Pray write, pray write, pray write"

## MC to TJ, 23 Dec. 1788

My Dear Friend

Give me leave to present you Mrs: [Hannah] Cowley the first femal dramatic Author in this Country,[22] she has most distinguishd talents, she is the most elegant writer, great poet, and a great Genius, a particular friend of mine and an amiable woman. You have I hope some frindship for me, speak of me with Mrs: Cowley. You will like her, take care of your heart, she may run away with it. How [I] envy her and every body that can converse with you: pray write, pray write, pray write, and dont go to America without coming to England.

God bless you and believe me Your Most affte frind

M.C.

---

[21] "From Thomas Jefferson to Maria Cosway, 26 September 1788," *Founders Online*, National Archives, https://founders.archives.gov/documents/Jefferson/01-13-02-0513. [Original source: *The Papers of Thomas Jefferson*, vol. 13, *March–7 October 1788*, ed. Julian P. Boyd. Princeton: Princeton University Press, 1956, pp. 638–639.]

[22] Hannah Cowley (1743–1809) was an English playwright and poet. Her plays were widely produced in her lifetime.

Chapter IV

# The Year 1789

Jefferson's last year in Paris, 1789, is busy. On April 30, George Washington becomes the first president of the fledgling country, with John Adams as his vice president. On September 11, Alexander Hamilton will be appointed as secretary of the treasury.

While things concretize in America with its new constitution and its first president, things in France become bedlamic. On July 14, Parisians storm the Bastille and release the few prisoners in it. That marks the provenance of the tumultuous French Revolution—so celebrated by Jefferson in its early days. As the revolution persists, there is more chaos and bloodshed.

Jefferson leaves Paris on September 26 and returns to Virginia on November 23. In the meantime, President Washington asks Jefferson to be his Secretary of State, and Jefferson, eager to return to Paris, will grudgingly accept early in 1790. Prior to Christmas Eve, he, Martha, Maria, and James and Sally Hemings return to Monticello. He is never again to return to France.

In the middle of January 1789, Jefferson resumes his correspondence with Cosway. The missive is very business-like, and Jefferson ends with resignation. He asks for a little corner of her affection in exchange for the large part she occupies in his affection. The correspondence hereafter is less intimate and becomes mostly an exchange of information between two friends. Cosway writes four letters this year; Jefferson, five.

### "A little corner of your affection"
### TJ to MC, Paris, 14 Jan. 1789

Fearing, my dear Madam, that I might not be able to write to you by this occasion, I had charged my friend Trumbull to lay my homage at your feet. But this is an office I would always chuse to perform myself. It is very long since I have heard from you: tho I have no right to complain, as it is long since I wrote to you. A great deal of business, and some tribulation must be my excuse. I have for two months past had a very sick family, and have not as yet a tranquil mind on that score.

How have you weathered this rigorous season, my dear friend? Surely it was never so cold before. To me who am an animal of a warm climate, a mere Oran-ootan, it has been a severe trial. Yet we have been generally cheered by the presence of the sun, of whose *bright* company at least you have been deprived. The weather has cut off communication between friends and acquaintances here.

I have seen the princess Lubomirski but once since her return, and Dancarville not this age. So that I am not able to give you any account of them. But they being more punctual correspondents than myself, have, I expect, given you an account of themselves. It is some time since I heard from Mde. de Brehan, and am sorry to tell you that by what I have heard she is furiously displeased with America. Her love of simplicity, and her wish to find it had made her fancy she was going to Arcadia, in spite of all my warnings to the contrary. My last letter from Mr. Short was dated at Rome. The poetical ground he was treading had almost filled him also with the god.

Have you arranged all things for the voiage with Mrs. Church? We are so apt to believe what we wish that I almost believe I shall meet you in America, and that we shall make together the tour of the curiosities of that country. Be this as it may, let us be together in spirit. Preserve for me always a little corner in your affection in exchange for the spacious part you occupy in mine. Adieu ma chere et tres chere amie! Yours respectfully & affectionately,

Th: J.[1]


Cosway replies some three weeks later. It is an unhappy letter, but she does not scold. She wonders why Jefferson will not stop in London and when he plans to return to America.

### "You seem to say so much in few words"
### MC to TJ, London, 6 Feb. 1789

London 6 Feb:

I thank you for your last letter, My dear friend, it is short, tho' a long while indeed writing, but you give me such reasons for your silence that I must forgive it, but it is with reluctance. You are going to America, and you think I am going with you, I thank you for the flattering compliment, I deserve it for I shall certainly be with you in spirit, I shall walk thro' the beautifull acres you will describe to me by letter; you shall share my envy between Mrs: Church and you, for I envy both excessively for the reciprocal pleasure you will have in one anothers Company; and your return when is it to be? Why dont you announce me that, as well as your departure? T'is

---

[1] "From Thomas Jefferson to Maria Cosway, 14 January 1789," *Founders Online,* National Archives, https://founders.archives.gov/documents/Jefferson/01-14-02-0216. [Original source: *The Papers of Thomas Jefferson,* vol. 14, *8 October 1788-26 March 1789,* ed. Julian P. Boyd. Princeton: Princeton University Press, 1958, pp. 445–446.]

cruel not to do it and you will not absolutely give us any hope of a visit here, how easy you Might do it! Why wont you, forget all the objections you May have [against England], and only think of those friends whose happiness you would Make by such an effort and sacrifice for them. I agree with you in Many things regarding a thousand objections against the caprices of this nation, I am disgusted by them day to day. Self-interested sentiments, selfishness in politics, with scandal which reigns without the least regard for personages, circumstances, humanity, and right or wrong: you cannot believe in this moment how much has been explained by a number of black and malicious hearts in the present state of politics; of the things published daily, intrigues, calumnies, and injustices in which all comment as if in a contest to see who can have superiority by force of atrocities, self-interest, and the least one thinks of seems to be the good of the nation. Oh why am I never to achieve my great desire of finding myself in solitude with a small number of friends? That is the only happiness, it lightens a great deal the way to the unhappiness felt in a crowd which one despises and makes longed for solitude full of every pleasure. One lives without knowledge of evil and enjoys the good without disturbance.

Shall I have the pleasure of hearing from you soon[?] I complain of the shortness of your letters, but it is only on the first glance in the paper, but when I read, you seem to say so much in few words that I forget the little number of the Cillabels [syllables] for the beauty of the expressions and elegant style. But I do wrong to say these things, you will despise me and think me a flatterer. I sent you a letter by Mrs. Cowley I hope you have seen her. How do you like her? Talk of me with her, she is sometimes too partial but she is a friend of Mine a woman of great genius and abilities and I love her and estime her much. God bless you my good friend continue your friendship to your

M.C—[2]

Jefferson's next letter is not till May, but he is preoccupied in readying himself, his daughters, and his two servants for travel across the ocean.

### "My absence will be of about six months"

## TJ to MC, Paris, 21 May 1789

I have not yet, my dear friend, received my leave of absence, but I expect it hourly, and shall depart almost in the hour of receiving it. My absence will be

---

[2] "To Thomas Jefferson from Maria Cosway, 6 February 1789," *Founders Online*, National Archives, https://founders.archives.gov/documents/Jefferson/01-14-02-0291. [Original source: *The Papers of Thomas Jefferson*, vol. 14, *8 October 1788-26 March 1789*, ed. Julian P. Boyd. Princeton: Princeton University Press, 1958, pp. 525–526.]

of about six months. I leave here a scene of tumult and contest. All is politics in this capital. Even love has lost it's part in conversation. This is not well, for love is always a consolatory thing. I am going to a country where it is felt in it's sublimest degree. In great cities it is distracted by the variety of objects. Friendship perhaps suffers there also from the same cause but I am determined to except from this your friendship for m[e], and to beleive it distracted by neither time, distance, nor object. When wafting on the bosom of the ocean I shall pray it to be as calm and smooth as yours to me.

What shall I say for you to our friend Mrs. Church? I shall see her assuredly, perhaps return with her. We shall talk a great deal of you. In fact you ought to have gone with her. We would have travelled a great deal together, we would have intruded our opinions into the choice of objects for your pencil and returned fraught with treasures of art, science and sentiment.

Adieu, my very dear friend. Be our affections unchangeable, and if our little history is to last beyond the grave, be the longest chapter in it that which shall record their purity, warmth and duration.[3]

Two months later, Jefferson again writes to Cosway.

### "The cutting off of heads has become so much à la mode..."
## TJ to MC, Paris, 25 July 1789

My letter of May 21. my dear Madam, was the last I expected to have written you on this side the Atlantic for the present year. Reasons, which I cannot devine, have prevented my yet receiving my Congé.

In the mean time we have been here in the midst of tumult and violence. The cutting off heads is become so much á la mode, that one is apt to feel of a morning whether their own is on their shoulders. Whether this work is yet over, depends on their catching more of the fugitives. If no new capture re-excites the spirit of vengeance, we may hope it will soon be at rest, and that order and safety will be reestablished except for a few of the most obnoxious characters. My fortune has been singular, to see in the course of fourteen years two such revolutions as were never before seen. But why should I talk of wars and revolutions to you who are all peace and goodness.

---

[3] "From Thomas Jefferson to Maria Cosway, 21 May 1789," *Founders Online*, National Archives, https://founders.archives.gov/documents/Jefferson/01-15-02-0140. [Original source: *The Papers of Thomas Jefferson*, vol. 15, *27 March 1789–30 November 1789*, ed. Julian P. Boyd. Princeton: Princeton University Press, 1958, pp. 142–143.]

Receive then into your peace and grace the bearer hereof Mr. Morris [Figure 4-1],[4] a countryman and friend of mine of great consideration in his own country, and who deserves to be so every where. Peculiarly gifted with fancy and judgment, he will be qualified to taste the beauties of your canvas. The Marquis de la Luzerne, an old and intimate acquaintance of his, will bear witness to you of his merit. But do not let him nestle me out of my place; for I still pretend to have one in your affection, tho' it is a long time since you told me so. I must soon begin to scold, if I do not hear from you. In order to be quiet, I persuade myself that you have thought me in, on, or over the Deep. But wherever I am, I feed on your friendship. I therefore need assurances of it in all times and places. Accept in return those which flow cordially from the heart of Your

Th: Jefferson[5]

Cosway fashions a short letter about six weeks after Jefferson's.

### "I did long Most excessively for a letter from you"
## MC to TJ, London, 9 Aug. 1789

I recive this Moment Your kind letter, by Mr. Morris, I thank you much. I did long Most excessivly for a letter from you. Mr: Trumbull is Coming to Paris. I have only as he will tell you half a moment to say *this* little but I will write a longer letter very soon. *En attend* believe me yours Most affly.,

M.C.[6]

---

[4] Gouverneur Morris (1752–1816)—a handsome playboy with a wooden leg, large conceit, and hifalutin ways—is a Federalist. He will be Jefferson's replacements in Paris. He will work his way into the company of the Cosways, while in London. His diary, which catalogs his numerous tristes, has many references to the goings on at the Cosways' salon.

[5] "From Thomas Jefferson to Maria Cosway, 21 May 1789," *Founders Online*, National Archives, https://founders.archives.gov/documents/Jefferson/01-15-02-0140. [Original source: *The Papers of Thomas Jefferson*, vol. 15, *27 March 1789–30 November 1789*, ed. Julian P. Boyd. Princeton: Princeton University Press, 1958, pp. 142–143.]

[6] "To Thomas Jefferson from Maria Cosway, 9 August 1789," *Founders Online*, National Archives, https://founders.archives.gov/documents/Jefferson/01-15-02-0328. [Original source: *The Papers of Thomas Jefferson*, vol. 15, *27 March 1789–30 November 1789*, ed. Julian P. Boyd. Princeton: Princeton University Press, 1958, p. 339.]

**Figure 4-1:** John Henry Hintermeister, *Foundation of American Government*, 1925

Source: Wikipedia

Cosway again writes on August 19. After some introductory comments, the letter reads like a bullet list, suggestive of it being written in haste.

### "My letters must appear sad scrawls to you"
## MC to TJ, London, 19 Aug. 1789

I owe you a letter, for the short one I sent by Mr. Trumbull, has not cleard my debt to you, and not satisfied my pleasure.

I wish always to converse longer with you. But when I read Your letters they are so well, wrote, so full of a thousand preaty things that it is not possible for me to Answer such charming letters. I could say many things if My pen could write exactly My sentiments and feelings, but my letters must appear sad scrawls to you. If I could fil them with interesting news at least but I have Nothing from this Country.

There has been an extraordinary Anecdote in one of the papers, but t'is either not beleaved, or not understood, nobody can make any thing of it; a discovery which has been made of a conspiracy against the King, the person are not named tho the number is mentioned being three and the possession of papers that would explain and unfold the whole. It Makes a noise, but I suppose that in time we shall know More about it.

I am quite in Love with Mr: Morris. Are all americans so engaging as those I know? Pray take me to that Country. Your description has long made me wish to see it, and the people I know confirm my desire.

I wish in your return to france you would come to England, since You will not in your way to America. T'is very cruel of you.

I wish you would send me some account of their affairs in France. T'is so difficult to have true news. We read and hear thousands.

Pray prepare a large parcel for the return of my Brother or Mr: Trumbull. They will be safe. Give me leave to present my Brother to you. I cannot speak of him if he deserve to be taken notice by you for I Can only speak with all the partiality of an affectionate Sister.

I hear Mr. Short is returnd. What does he say of Italy? Pray give My Compliments to him.

Mr. Cosway joins with me in Compliments to both. Believe always your Most affte:

Maria Cosway[7]

Part of the intendment of the letter is to introduce her brother George Hadfield to Jefferson so that the latter might be of assistance to the young man in advancing his situation in America. Jefferson, who claims ever to be averse to cronyism,[8] will do what he can do to assist the young man, for he willingly assists "every man of talents, and particularly every one connected with you."

Jefferson's subsequent letter expresses certain misunderstandings and certain albatrosses concerning attempts to meet George Hadfield.

### "Were there a hope of meeting you here on my return…"
### TJ to MC, Paris, 11 Sept. 1789

My dear Madam

I have been very unfortunate in my endeavors to see more of your brother who was so good as to call on me with your letter. I wrote to ask him to come and dine with me. Unfortunately there was an American in the same hotel whose name had some resemblance to that on the superscription of my letter, and a French porter delivered my note to him instead of your brother. A sickness then confined me a week to my room. The day before yesterday, being the first day on which I

---

[7] "To Thomas Jefferson from Maria Cosway, 19 August 1789," *Founders Online*, National Archives, https://founders.archives.gov/documents/Jefferson/01-15-02-0344. [Original source: *The Papers of Thomas Jefferson*, vol. 15, *27 March 1789-30 November 1789*, ed. Julian P. Boyd. Princeton: Princeton University Press, 1958, p. 351.]

[8] E.g., TJ to George Jefferson, 27 Mar. 1801, and TJ to John Garland Jefferson, 25 Jan. 1810.

could write, I wrote again an invitation to him to come and dine with me. The answer was from the hotel that he had left that, they did not know whether for the country, or for England, so that I am deprived of the opportunity of shewing him how much I esteem every man of talents, and particularly every one connected with you. I must pray you to become my apologist to him and the organ of my regrets.

Tho' neither the day of my departure, nor the vessel by which I go be yet fixed, the necessity of being ready to go at a moment's warning, induces me to scribble you a line of Adieu, while it is yet in my power. Preserve for me always, my dear friend, the same sentiments of esteem you have been so good as to entertain for me hitherto. They will comfort me in going, and encourage me returning. Were there a hope of meeting you here on my return the encouragement would be complete. I count certainly to be here in the month of May. It is a charming month, and should tempt you also to travel. By that time too this country will be in perfect freedom and tranquillity, and even without that, you will be free and tranquil every where.

Adieu my dear friend; protect me with your prayers and quiet me with your affection.[9]

In Cosway's reply, the coquette is absent. She instead expresses sincere desire to see Jefferson before he departs for America.

### "Every difficulty opposes my desire of surprising you with a visit"

## MC to TJ, London, 9 Oct. 1789

I did not answer your last letter, my dear friend, because I was in doubt whether it would find you at Paris, but now I shall profit of Mr: Trumbuls departure to send you a line to put you in Mind of me in those still more distant parts of the Globe, where your friends perhaps all your heart and sentiments are. It will be very flattering to me if you think of me some times. I was very near coming to see you when Trumbull told me that you was to be at the Isle of White [Wight], but I have been very ill with a Most violent Cold. The weather is very bad, and every difficulty opposes my desire of surprising you with a visit, but why dont you come. It would be so easy so short, and such pleasure to us. I think I could

---

[9] "From Thomas Jefferson to Maria Cosway, 11 September 1789," *Founders Online*, National Archives, https://founders.archives.gov/documents/Jefferson/01-15-02-0399. [Original source: *The Papers of Thomas Jefferson*, vol. 15, *27 March 1789–30 November 1789*, ed. Julian P. Boyd. Princeton: Princeton University Press, 1958, pp. 413–414.]

be Angry with you for not Coming, but perhaps you Cannot. You may have your reasons therefore [I] shall say no more.

I will not take more of your time up now but expect a longer letter when you tell me where to write. I am so ill at present I cannot write More. Beleave always I shall be your most affte.

M. Cosway[10]

While Jefferson is detained at Cowes due to unfavorable winds to cross the English Channel *en route* to America, Trumbull meets up with Jefferson and brings to him a letter from Cosway. While waiting for propitious weather, Jefferson pens the last letter of the year 1789 between the two.

### "A meeting at Paris with the first swallow"
### TJ to MC, Cowes, 14 Oct. 1789

I am here, my dear friend, waiting the arrival of a ship to take my flight from this side of the Atlantic and as we think last of those we love most, I profit of the latest moment to bid you a short but affectionate Adieu. Before this, Trumbull will have left you: but we are more than exchanged by Mrs. Church who will probably be with you in the course of the present month. My daughters are with me and in good health. We have left a turbulent scene, and I wish it may be tranquilized on my return, which I count will be in the month of April. Under present circumstances, aggravated as you will read them in the English papers, we cannot hope to see you in France. But a return of quiet and order may remove that bugbear, and the ensuing spring might give us a meeting at Paris with the first swallow.

So be it, my dear friend, and Adieu under the hope which springs naturally out of what we wish. Once and again then farewell, remember me and love me.[11]

---

[10] To Thomas Jefferson from Maria Cosway, 9 October 1789," *Founders Online*, National Archives, https://founders.archives.gov/documents/Jefferson/01-15-02-0490. [Original source: *The Papers of Thomas Jefferson*, vol. 15, *27 March 1789–30 November 1789*, ed. Julian P. Boyd. Princeton: Princeton University Press, 1958, pp. 513–514.]

[11] "From Thomas Jefferson to Maria Cosway, 14 October 1789," *Founders Online*, National Archives, https://founders.archives.gov/documents/Jefferson/01-15-02-0498. [Original source: *The Papers of Thomas Jefferson*, vol. 15, *27 March 1789-30 November 1789*, ed. Julian P. Boyd. Princeton: Princeton University Press, 1958, p. 521.]

Chapter V

# The Years 1790 to 1805

With Jefferson's departure to America—he, of course, has with him his daughters Martha and Maria and slaves James and Sally Hemings—the two will never again meet. Jefferson arrives at Norfolk and stops at Eppington—the plantation home of brother-in-law Francis Eppes—on his way to Monticello. He receives a missive there—another is sent to Monticello—from George Washington, who requests his acceptance of the post of Secretary of State in the first president's administration.

Jefferson will accept the post of secretary of state, suffer a brief retirement from politics during President Washington's second term, and then assume the vice presidency and then the presidency of the United States—the last, for two terms. On February 23, 1790, daughter Martha weds Thomas Mann Randolph. On October 13, 1797, daughter Maria weds Francis Eppes' son, John Wayles Eppes. In 1797, Jefferson becomes president of the American Philosophical Society—a post he shall hold for 18 years.

Key events of Jefferson's first term as president include declaration of war on Tripoli (6 Feb. 1802), repeal of Judiciary Act (8 Mar. 1802), opening of West Point Military Academy (4 July 1802), passage of Louisiana Enabling Act (31 Oct. 1803), death of daughter Maria (17 Apr. 1804), beginning of Lewis and Clark Expedition (14 May 1804), and the death of Alexander Hamilton (11 July 1804), and a peace treaty with Tripoli (4 June 1805).

The Cosways, meanwhile, have a daughter, Louisa Paolina Angelica Cosway,[1] born in 1790. The child will live only till 1796. Cosway's recovery after delivery will be hard and long. She will fall ill—intensified certainly by severe post-natal depression—and leave London for Italy, where she will remain without her daughter, who stays behind in London, for four years to convalesce.

Moreover, the mental instability of King George III can no longer be covered by the euphemisms of his friends, physicians, and flatterers. He is declared mad in 1790, and his son, the Prince of Wales, becomes Prince Regent. Cosway's residence, Schomburg House, is then frequented by Whigs, who have been blocking the regency of the prince, and so the prince breaks his ties with the

---

[1] "Louisa" after godmother, Louise de Stolbert; "Paolina" after godfather, General Paoli; and "Angelica" after Angelica Church.

Cosways—thereby attenuating the importance of Richard Cosway in England's high society.

After Jefferson's letter of October 1789, there is a lengthy respite, nearly six months, in their correspondence, which is ended by Cosway, who is soon to have a child.

There will be 10 letters exchanged between the two from 1790 to 1805—the *terminus ad quem* determined by an enormous gap after 1805. Cosway will write seven; Jefferson, three.

### "The greatest effort I can Make..."
## MC to TJ, London, 6 Apr. 1790

I fear My Dear freind has forgot me; Not One line ever Since your Departure from this part of the world! I have heard of you, tho' not from you. Dont let my reproches be too Severe for I am willing to think you have been prevented by important reasons. However Silence from a person who feels the privation of your letters, would be impossible. The greatest effort I can Make is a short letter, not to take up too Much of your time but to bring you to recolection an affectionate freind in

Maria Cosway[2]

If ever you see Mr. Trumbull I hope you will speak of me together. I shall be happy to have my name breathed up by the delightfull air of your Country among the charms of friendship hospitality and many other qualities it possesses, and which I wish I could admire in *persona* as well as I do at a distance.

Jefferson, in readiness for his post as secretary of state, replies some 11 weeks later from New York City.

### "Que vous allez faire un enfant"
## TJ to MC, New York, 23 June 1790

I received, my dear friend, your favor of Apr. 6. It gives me a foretaste of the sensations we are to feel in the next world, on the arrival of any new-comer from the circle of friends we have left behind.

---

[2] "To Thomas Jefferson from Maria Cosway, 6 April 1790," *Founders Online*, National Archives, https://founders.archives.gov/documents/Jefferson/01-16-02-0182. [Original source: *The Papers of Thomas Jefferson*, vol. 16, *30 November 1789–4 July 1790*, ed. Julian P. Boyd. Princeton: Princeton University Press, 1961, pp. 312–313.]

I am now fixed here, and look back to Europe only on account of that circle. Could it be transferred here, the measure of all I could desire in this world would be filled up, for I have no desire but to enjoy the affections of my heart, which are divided now by a wide sea.

You know I always ranted about your bringing your pencil and harp here. They would go well with our groves, our birds, and our sun. Trumbull is painting away but being at Philadelphia I cannot have the solace of talking with him about you.

They tell me *que vous allez faire un enfant. Je vous en felicite de tout mon coeur*.[3] This will wean you from your harp and your pencil, by filling your heart with joys still more bewitching. You may make children there, but this is the country to transplant them to. There is no comparison between the sum of happiness enjoyed here and there. All the distractions of your great Cities are but feathers in the scale against the domestic enjoiments and rural occupations, and neighborly societies we live amidst here. I summon you then as a mother to come and join us. You must tell me you will, whether you mean it, or no.

*En attendant je vous aimerai toujours.*[4] Adieu, my Dear Maria, Yours affectionately,

Th: Jefferson[5]

The principal motivation for the letter is to felicitate Cosway for her child-to-be, though he is unaware that the child is born on May 4. He again tries to lure her, with child, to visit America and its groves, birds, and sun. "You may make children there, but this is the country to transplant them to." If she places into a scale the domestic enjoyments and rural occupations of America and the "distractions of your great Cities," the latter will seem to be feathers. He ends by noting that he will always love her.

Cosway will be in Italy without her daughter for four years—she will be recovering from her difficult pregnancy—and will only return to London in 1794. She writes of that dubious time in her autobiographical letter to Sir William Cosway (1830):

---

[3] Note that Jefferson uses the unfamiliar *vous* and not the familiar *tu*.
[4] "In the meantime, I shall ever love you," and again the unfamiliar *vous* is employed, suggesting of a love between good friends, not intimates.
[5] "From Thomas Jefferson to Maria Cosway, 23 June 1790," *Founders Online*, National Archives, https://founders.archives.gov/documents/Jefferson/01-16-02-0321. [Original source: *The Papers of Thomas Jefferson*, vol. 16, *30 November 1789–4 July 1790*, ed. Julian P. Boyd. Princeton: Princeton University Press, 1961, pp. 550–551.]

> I had only one child a little girl I had [a] bad time & a worse confinement so that my life was in danger the Physicians agreed change of Air. Lady Wright was going to Italy for the health of her son, my brother George Hadfield had gained the Gold Medal & sent by the Academy to Rome—Mr. Cosway bought me a Carriage—with my Maid & my brother we travelled with Lady Wright by my health so bad I could not go to Rome—as soon as recovered I wrote to Mr. C. I was ready to return he kept me from Spring to Autumn for almost three years as he meant to come himself. But being suddenly taken ill I travelled night & day in the midst of War & dangers in the Month of November got home safe & had the satisfaction of finding Mr. C. recovered, and a fine little girl to engage all my cares & occupations. All my friends saw me again with infinite pleasure—for two years I had the pleasure of seeing my child grow & profit of my education—she was seized by a sore throat & in the sixth year of age we lost her—our grief was great. I returned to painting.[6]

That is, of course, Cosway's account, succinct and somewhat incoherent. Is she really in danger of her life? Does she really need four years to recover?

It is extraordinary to think that Cosway, however ill, can convalesce without being with her new daughter. That has not gone unnoticed by those acquainted with Cosway. Londoner Horace Walpole—writer, critic, and politician—writes in a letter to Agnes and Mary Berry, who are in Florence, "I used to call Mrs. Cosway's concerts Charon's boat, now methinks London is so. I am glad she is with you; she is pleasing—but surely it is odd to drop a child and her husband and her country all in a breath."[7] Londoner Hester Lynch Thrale Piozzi—Welsh diarist, patron of the arts, and writer—notes in her journal (29 Mar. 1794): "When Mrs. Cosway ran madding all over Europe after a Castrato, leaving her husband & new-born Baby at home here: She was praying at the foot of every Altar & fasting most rigorously all the time—a hypocritical Hussey! … Her Faith is not influenced by her Actions I suppose; She was well persuaded of heavenly Truths, altho' a Prey to almost infernal Passions: or Appetites strangely depraved."[8]

Walpole's letter and Piozzi's journal typify the scandalmongery that was circulating in London concerning Cosway, who is at the time seen with the celebrated singer Luigi Marchesi (1754–1829, Figure 5-1). What overall seems

---

[6] Gerald Barnett, "Appendix VI," *Richard and Maria Cosway: A Biography* (Cambridge: The Lutterworth Press, 1995), 261.
[7] Helen Duprey Bullock, *My Head and My Heart: A Little History of Thomas Jefferson and Maria Cosway* (New York: G.P. Putnam's Sons, 1945), 136.
[8] Carol Burnell, *Divided Affections*, 269.

clear is that any affection Maria might have had for Richard has evanesced. "It seems odd that she could abandon her young child, but a difficult pregnancy, marital unhappiness, and postnatal illness had prevented a bond from establishing itself between her and Louisa."⁹ One can add that disdain for London, which next to Paris or Florence is almost oppressively dreary, adds to her desire for separation.

**Figure 5-1:** Richard Cosway, Portrait of Luigi Marchesi, 1790

Source: National Portrait Gallery, London

Unlike George Williamson and Gerald Barnett, who gloss over all scandalmongery concerning Maria Cosway,[10] Burnell maintains that Cosway stays with Luigi Marchesi from the autumn of 1791 to the autumn of 1792 at his

---

[9] Carol Burnell, *Divided Affections: The Extraordinary Life of Maria Cosway: Celebrity Artist and Thomas Jefferson's Impossible Love* (London: Column House, 2007), 274. More a more detailed account, see chapter 14 of Burnell's book.
[10] Barnett calls it "abusive publicity" that is not "very different from that which governs our own gutter tabloids," while Williamson merely notes lack of evidence for any salaciousness and existence of "very much indeed [that] lead me to hold an exactly opposite opinion of her life," though he fails to expand. George Williamson, *Richard Cosway, R.A.*, 49, and Gerald Barnett, *Richard and Maria Cosway*, 112.

residence in Milan. She is before in residence in Florence.[11] Does she have a sexual affair with the castrato? We do not know. Castration is not necessarily a signal of incapacity of sexual performance, but there is nothing in Cosway's papers to show or even suggest any intimacy. Nevertheless, most intimate communications—familial letters and those letters from Jefferson and Marchesi—have been destroyed, so we perhaps shall never know.[12]

Yet in September 1792, Cosway leaves Milan and Marchesi to enter a Genoan convent suggestive of compunction. She has known London's Genoan ambassador, Francesco d'Ageno, but being an Englishwoman who has married a Protestant, the nuns are reluctant to accept her. She is finally accepted to the Convent of Santa Brigida, run by the Order of the Visitation as is Il Conventino in Florence, with the aid of a prominent Genoan, but merely to assume the cloistered life of a retired woman, not a nun. Burnell states that "this separation from the brilliant world ... was not painful in the least," but "corresponded to her innermost desires." Her marriage is in shambles—she has written Richard Cosway on many occasions to ask for forgiveness, but her husband does not respond—and so she wishes to retreat from the world but in doing so, asks him for an annual allowance of 60 pounds. She will remain in the convent, where she was allowed contact with the world outside, for some 18 months.

Maria Cosway sends her maid Madison to London along with a letter to tell Richard Cosway of her intentions. "Whatever I may have done to displease, I again ask your forgiveness as I have done before in one of my letters to which I have had no answer." She continues: "I have not wrote for some time because there have been so many troubles & differences about the convents that it has taken all this time. The first difficulty has been for being married to a protestant and being a stranger & married. The nuns are so exceedingly ignorant & prejudiced that it is impossible to make them understand common sense."[13] The last sentence is evidence that her retreat will not result in a comfortable subsistence at any convent, but her intention is certainly to escape reality and, once again, to repent for whatever transgressions she may have committed. It cannot be the case that her separation from the world, à la Burnell, is "not painful in the least." It is instead what Cosway considers for the nonce to be the least painful option. She cannot remain with Marchesi, so she must retire among the ignorant and prejudiced nuns, as she did when she was young.

Cosway continues in her letter to her husband about her twin concerns: money and her daughter. She mentions the gossip concerning how she has

---

[11] Carol Burnell, *Divided Affections*, 274.
[12] Carol Burnell, *Divided Affections*, 469.
[13] Carol Burnell, *Divided Affections*, 278.

come to her money and the worry that once in a convent, Richard "may not continue [his] remittance." She adds: "The child is my only wish & thought, & my fears only for her religion, from her first impressions depend on her sentiment of the true faith ... the pure catholic." She ends, "I hope the child is well may God protect her."[14] Reference to her daughter as "the child" and not by her Christian name is strongly suggestive of a lack of deep affection for the girl. The worry for the child is that if not brought up as Catholic, her daughter might be damned in the afterlife.

Jefferson hears of Cosway's retirement and writes of that incredible turn of life in a letter to Angelica Schuyler Church (27 Nov. 1793): "And Madame Cosway in a convent! I knew that, to much goodness of heart, she joined enthusiasm and religion: but I thought that very enthusiasm would have prevented her from shutting up her adoration of the god of the Universe within the walls of a cloyster; that she would rather have sought the *mountain-top.*"[15]

Cosway's decision to leave Milan for a cloistered life in Genoa follows her recurrent pattern of need to sin and of need to confess and repent. Sinning is exhilarating, but when overdone, one is left feeling empty and dreadful, and one endures the emptiness and dread through confession and repentance. It is a cycle from which Cosway cannot escape. That is not to say that Cosway has consummated an affair with Marchesi but merely that she harbors compunction from her peccability. She has, after all, left behind her husband and her child so that she might "convalesce."

While Maria Cosway is away, Richard Cosway begins an affair with artist Mary Moser, recently jilted by artist Henry Fuseli. The two travel on a six-month "sketching tour" in 1793. Richard writes openly of the lascivious affair with Moser in his journal, where he talks, among other things, of her being more sexually responsive than his wife.[16] Of that journal, Richard's early biographer, George Williamson, writes:

> The two artists, each of them over fifty years of age, were nominally travelling on a sketching tour, but Cosway, in a rough, disjointed manner records in a sort of diary the incidents of their journey, alternating the

---

[14] Carol Burnell, *Divided Affections*, 279.
[15] "From Thomas Jefferson to Angelica Schuyler Church, 27 November 1793," *Founders Online*, National Archives, https://founders.archives.gov/documents/Jefferson/01-27-02-0416. [Original source: *The Papers of Thomas Jefferson*, vol. 27, *1 September–31 December 1793*, ed. John Catanzariti. Princeton: Princeton University Press, 1997, pp. 449–450.]
[16] Andrea Fernandes, "Scandalous Academician: Mary Moser," *Mental Floss*, https://www.mentalfloss.com/article/23116/scandalous-academician-mary-moser, accessed 7 September 2022.

entries with sketches of the places they visited. The drawings are delightful, but the journal will not bear repetition, as it is confined almost exclusively to lascivious statements about Miss Moser, and invidious comparisons between her and Mrs. Cosway.[17]

Williamson, noting that Richard Cosway's journal has been found among the papers she kept and preserved, asserts that Maria knows of the triste and forgives her husband on account of her "deep affection for her husband and love to him."[18] That seems most improbable. She has certainly been privy to Richard's indiscretions for many years—she has perhaps participated in some of them—and his behavior comes as no surprise, so there is no reason for deep-felt animosity. It is impossible to hate someone whom one no longer in any degree loves. Again, the preservation of his diary among her papers might be for historical revenge. Future scholars will discover the journal and write about his libertinism.

Independently of his triste with Moser, Richard Cosway's life in London is drastically altered. The absence of his wife leads to gossip of all sorts. It is impossible to host musical evenings of the same caliber without Maria, and Richard's social circle is clearly much narrower. Schomberg House is "a place of echoes." Nonetheless, Richard has time to devote to his craft. There is "a heightened quality to his painting and drawing as the volume of his commerce decreased." His miniatures are especially outstanding.[19]

Desiring long for a return home, Maria Cosway finally heads back to London, on hearing, through letters from her siblings, of Richard's desire that she return home—he has presumably also taken ill—and then receiving in confirmation the same information from her husband. "I thought it proper to wait for your letters because I know how *we were*. ... My Mother's letters nor my Brother's were sufficient for me to precipitate at their imitation."[20] She stops in Paris and gets a first-hand impression of the sanguinary revolution. Upon her arrival in London, she writes a letter to be forwarded by Trumbull to Jefferson. When she arrives, she finds that they no longer occupy Schomberg House but have moved to a new residence off Oxford Street. It is then that she discovers the four-year-old letter of Jefferson. While suffering from compunction, she knows that a

---

[17] George C. Williamson, *Richard Cosway, R.A.* (London: George Bell and Sons, 1905), 50–51. The journal that Williamson inspected cannot today be located. Gerald Barnett, *Richard and Maria Cosway: A Biography* (Cambridge: The Lutterworth Press, 1995), 125.
[18] George C. Williamson, *Richard Cosway, R.A.*, 51.
[19] Gerald Barnett, *Richard and Maria Cosway*, 129–30.
[20] Gerald Barnett, "Appendix VI," *Richard and Maria Cosway*, 261.

letter from Jefferson, who preaches the gospel that happiness is virtuous industry, is a fine Catholicon. She replies with a short letter.

### "T'is impossible to express my happiness"
### MC to TJ, London, 13 Nov. 1794

My Dear Sir

I am come home to England, and have the great pleasure to find I am not forgoten by Mr: Jefferson, t'is impossible to express my happiness, the less I say the better, and am Sure what I dont say will be added by a Heart who can conceive and interpatrate [interpret] Sentiments of a feeling and greatfull heart. My Angelica [Church] has been the greatest joy on my return. She has flatterd me much by telling me my name was mentiond in most of the letters which come from America. Mr: Trumbull tells me the Same and offers to send a letter; Now I have Not time to make One, till now I did Not know how to send one, but hope that I shall in another find more to convince You how much I am your Most Affte.

Maria Cosway[21]

Eleven days later, a repenting Cosway pens another letter, much longer, to Jefferson. It is in her periods of repentancy that she most thinks of Jefferson, and that is extraordinarily meaningful.

### "I have found a preaty little girl"
### MC to TJ, London, 24 Nov. 1794

Dear Sir

I sent you a very short letter On My Arrival here, but promised Soon a longer One, here I am ready for it, from a great wish to converse a little with One whom ought to be my freind from a simpathy of Sentiments: You know this does not Mean that the easons [for sympathy of sentiments] are the same, Mine may be raised by the Consciousness of your Merits, in that case I have nothing to pretend from you, but you May then return some acknowledgement built only

---

[21] "To Thomas Jefferson from Maria Cosway, 13 November 1794," *Founders Online*, National Archives, https://founders.archives.gov/documents/Jefferson/01-28-02-0143. [Original source: *The Papers of Thomas Jefferson*, vol. 28, *1 January 1794–29 February 1796*, ed. John Catanzariti. Princeton: Princeton University Press, 2000, p. 201.]

on a sort of gratitude that will mingle the tenderness of freindship, forgit from what source it Comes, and be pure in its effect.

Mr: Trumbull told me a few days ago he had an opportunity of sending a Letter, but was prevented from sending to him One. Last Night Mrs: Church told me she has another; sure t'is Opportunities coming with a reproach when they are felt with so much pleasure, and at the same time as a reward for what Seems a negligence not embracing the first without a fault, a second recompences the sensearly felt loss. Now this will Come accompanied by One from the Most charming of woman, My Angelica [Church], I love her so much that I think and am persuaded she must be beloved by every One who know her, therefore give value to every thing which Comes from her Or she Notices with her regard. I will think she has Some attachment for me and I value it much. My great fear is that soon I shall loos her, I even thought I should not find her in England, but have been fortunate to meet this pleasure On my arrival, and certainly she was a great consolation to me. Could I but think it a lasting One, You know this Country, and believe you have heard My sentiments on it, My long stay in Italy and particularly the fine Climate and Most beautifull situation of Genova has Not alterd them but increased a surmontable Antipathy I feel, though the pleasure of the good society and amiable freinds Make in great Measure a recompence, t'is accompanied with a dampness of a gloomy cloud which withers the first blossom of the appearing charm, waits for some glimps of the raising sunn, and stops till t'is forgot in thought in Amazement, or indifference.

I often think of America, and every thing I hear of it pleases me and Makes me wish to come, why Can I not come? How Many things are like the Italians and Italy? There is a Comfort in freinds and their Society.

I have found a preaty little girl, I hope she will make some Comfort, she shows Natural Talent and a good, Soft disposition—painting and Musik for the present are forgotten by me, the long neglect has made me now give them up, and find no loss, better occupations will fill up My heavy hours.

Je vous fait Mon Compliment, et je vous suppose deja un gran Papa![22] May you have in every Circumstance of your life that happiness you so Much deserve, Much for the choise you Make of your happiness. Oh how few at this Moment! Where is there a smal spot unknown to Misery, trouble, and Confusion? You have retierd from it, but Much is the loss for those you Might have been of use to.

---

[22] "I send you my greetings, and I suspect that you are by now a grandfather."

Mr: Cosway desires his Compliments and joins with me in all I have said. He Might have wrote better English, but My wishes I will not give up to any body. Remember Me ever as one of your Most affte: friends

Maria Cosway[23]

Cosway, upon her return to London, finds her husband fully recovered, and as a penitent Catholic, she relinquishes the pleasures of painting and music for the duties of motherhood. Yet she articulates merely a "hope" that the "preaty little girl" will help her to "fill up [her] heavy hours," and her question concerning "a small spot unknown to Misery, trouble and Confusion" shows that her voluntary relinquishment is perhaps merely a short-term concession to moral dutifulness. It is noteworthy that Maria again does not refer to her child by name, once more intimating a distance between the two. Has she come to execrate so much her husband that she cannot even love a child that has come to be from the two of them?

Jefferson, at this time, is retired for a spell from public office and returns to Monticello to resume the agrarian lifestyle of an owner of a plantation. He will remain in retirement for a short time until republican duty will enjoin him to run for the U. S. presidency. In his next letter to Cosway, his first in over five years, he is zestful and reinvigorated, and his animation is kindled by retirement from the Augean tasks of politics. Surrounded by innocent scenes, Jefferson is inclined heretofore "to practice innocence towards all, hurt to none, [and] help to as many as I am able."

## "Where fancy submits all things to our will"
### TJ to MC, Monticello, 8 Sept. 1795

My dear Madam

Your two favors, sent thro' Mr. Trumbul, found me retired to my home, in the full enjoiment of my farm, my family, and my books, having bidden an eternal Adieu to public life which I always hated, and was drawn into and kept in by one of those great events which happened only once in a millenium as I thought, but another country has shewn us they can happen twice in a life.

---

[23] "To Thomas Jefferson from Maria Cosway, 24 November 1794," *Founders Online*, National Archives, https://founders.archives.gov/documents/Jefferson/01-28-02-0152. [Original source: *The Papers of Thomas Jefferson*, vol. 28, *1 January 1794–29 February 1796*, ed. John Catanzariti. Princeton: Princeton University Press, 2000, pp. 209–211.]

While my countrymen are making a great buz about Mr. Jay and his treaty with your adoptive country, I am eating the peaches, grapes and figs of my own garden and only wish I could taste them in your native country, gathered on the spot and in your good company.

I think you, Mrs. Church and myself must take a trip together to Italy, not forgetting Made. de Corny, tho she seems to have forgotten us, or some of us, for I have not had *de pas nouvelles* since I left France.

Having revisited Italy, I wonder you could leave it again for the smoke and rains of London. However you have the privilege of making fair weather wherever you go. I suppose that in our way to Italy it will be hardly worth our while to go through France. Our acquaintance there must be entirely dissipated. I think however we may venture by the route of Languedoc, and Nice. We shall have the pleasure of climbing the Cornice of the Riviera di Genoa together, and of seeing many romantic scenes to which your pencil and imagination would do justice. (The chateau di Saorgio, by the bye, is on the Col de Tende road.) But I wish to see Genoa again and bespoke some charming rooms there against my return.

We will leave the rest of the journey to imagination, and return to what is real.

I am become, for instance, a real farmer, measuring fields, following my ploughs, helping the haymakers, and never knowing a day which has not done something for futurity. How much better this than to be shut up in the four walls of an office, the sun of heaven excluded, the balmy breeze never felt, the evening closed with the barren consolation that the drudgery of the day is got through, the morning opening with the fable renewed of the Augean stable, a new load of labour in place of the old, and thus day after day worn through, with no prospect before us but of more days to wear through in the same way.

From such a life, good lord deliver me, and to such an one consign me only when the measure of thy wrath shall be completely filled! But it shall never be filled towards me as long as I am permitted, from the innocence of the scenes around me, to learn and to practice innocence towards all, hurt to none, help to as many as I am able.

but I am rambling again, my dear friend, and must recall myself to order. In truth whenever I think of you, I am hurried off on the wings of imagination into regions where fancy submits all things to our will. I had better therefore seat you soberly before a London coal-fire, walk out into the sun myself, tell him he does not shine on a being whose happiness I wish more than yours; pray him devoutly to bind his beams together with tenfold force, to penetrate if possible the mass of smoke and fog under which you are buried, and to gild with his rays the room you inhabit, and the road you travel: then tell you I have a most sincere and cordial friendship for you, that I regret the distance which separates us, and will not permit myself to believe we are no more to meet till you meet where time and distance are nothing. Your affectionate friend

Th: Jefferson[24]

Cosway writes three months later a philosophical letter to Jefferson.

### "The virtues we can practice, the vices we can avoid"
## MC to TJ, London, 4 Dec. 1795

Dear Sir

At last I have the long wished pleasure of receiving a letter from you? I cannot tell how much it has made me happy for I could not suspect you could forgit me, tho am sensible My not having sufficient Merit to engage your remembrance, but can only trust to the Sentiments known to me for so long a time and formed Upon So much Sure foundation. How glad am I to hear your detachment from the busling world, what is this world? Happy, very happy those who Make it a good passage to a better One, to an everlasting life, we can be very happy in this with these veiws of it for then we only think of the virtues we can practice, the vices we Can avoid, the end we are created for, the recompence is destind to us which no body can usurpe and when we act for the Omnipresent or Omnipotent who sees every thing how can we wish, or be disturb'd at the Momentary circumstances which pass like lightning to leave every thing in ashes.

You will soon have the pleasure of seeing the Charming Anjelica. I loose her with Much regret she is the woman I love Most, and feel Most happy with in this Country. Poor Madm. de Corney has met with a great Change in her life from what she was.

I wanted Much to send a letter to you by My brother George Hadfield but the resolution of his going away without taking leave prevented My knowing of his departure till he was gone, however I know You will be kind to all and need Not Say any thing particular for him. I hope he will meet with encouragement, he has talents and an amiable Character, tho he is my brother I must be just.

---

[24] "From Thomas Jefferson to Maria Cosway, 8 September 179[5]," *Founders Online*, National Archives, https://founders.archives.gov/documents/Jefferson/01-28-02-0357. [Original source: *The Papers of Thomas Jefferson*, vol. 28, *1 January 1794–29 February 1796*, ed. John Catanzariti. Princeton: Princeton University Press, 2000, pp. 455–456.]

You Mention Geneva in Your letter with satisfaction. Many thanks for I love it very Much as well as admire it. How happy I was there in those enchanting walls of the Most beautifull Situation. What a sound a Monastory is If all thought it the heaven I do, the world would end and the gospel obliged to alter its prediction. What a differance in this town in this bustling situation, from that solitude? Those bells who put me in Mind Constantly of our Maker our duties and our end, who united My Mind with angels and heaven. Here indeed the Crowns must be treeple [triple] and so they will be if recompance is to be according to difficulty and pain. My duties however are here and here I make My Crowns, my happiness in the will of God, a will which Must be done, let us follow it with Love.

I will not attempt to enter into political news or insignificant things. Theathers and Masquerades, assemblies Concerts and Cards, Shops and shows make all the occupation of these good people. My little girl, my pencil and my home make mine, and endevor to make my time very short by making it useful.

What would I give to surprize you on your Monticello!

I have Your picture by Troumbel on the side of my Chimney always before me, and always regret that perhaps never can I see the Original. At least if I could have oftner your letters t'would be some compensation, but to be deprived of both is too much.

Resolve and break this long intervals. Yours most affy:

M. Cosway[25]

Cosway's letter shows a Jeffersonian turn of disposition. She shuns prodigality for usefulness. Her occupations are now wholly domestic: her girl, her pencil, her home. She tells Jefferson that she has hung a copy of Trumbull's miniature of him (Figure 5-2) on the side of a chimney that always faces her. This letter, I maintain, marks maturation in Cosway. She has reconciled herself to the asceticism of domesticity, and with that reconciliation, she now longs for Jefferson—"What would I give to surprise you on your Monticello!"—as Jefferson once longed for her.

---

[25] "To Thomas Jefferson from Maria Cosway, 4 December 1795," *Founders Online*, National Archives, https://founders.archives.gov/documents/Jefferson/01-28-02-0421. [Original source: *The Papers of Thomas Jefferson*, vol. 28, *1 January 1794-29 February 1796*, ed. John Catanzariti. Princeton: Princeton University Press, 2000, pp. 543–544.]

**Figure 5-2:** John Trumbull, *Miniature of Jefferson*, 1788

Source: White House Historical Association

There is not another letter for four and one-half years, and it is Cosway who pens it to Jefferson, who is now president of the United States. In the interval, Cosway's daughter has died in 1796 from a throat ailment of some sort.

**"My letters may have lost the way of being acceptable"**

# MC to TJ, London, 20 July 1801

I must not look back to the date of our last Correspondence it would alarm & discourage me from taking the pen up this Moment. Your kindness to me has been of all times, & your friendship & mine took its date from its beggining: Circumstances, not your will I am sure have deprived me of the pleasure I used to value so much of receiving your letters. Many Many times my thoughts [are turned] towards you, with a wish to write. [...] a transition check'd my resolution [...] fears & doubts, it is unjust to suspect you & I wrong you my dear friend, why should I admit the Shadow of a thought that my letters may have lost the way of being acceptable, however perseivd by My imaginary Visions, several Motives crowd now to forward my [desires].

Would you not receive the congratulations of an old friend, qui vous ete sincerement devouée?[26] While you are surrownded by those of your Country, could you permit a thought that time or distance has at all lessend My interest in what attends you? this is enough: words cannot express all I should say on the subject. & you have so much of that sympathising sentiment to enable you to Conceive more than I can write what the occasion would require.

May God Continue to be your guide, as you have […] Service for the welfare of your Country & [the] happiness of your friends.

This letter was to have been presented to you by a friend of Mine who set out a Month ago, the Beli Ruspoli Brother to Prince Ruspoli of Rome as amiable as he is cleaver, travelling for his instruction as well as his pleasure. to know you was his wish, & mine to have comply'd with it, but his sudden departure prevented him Coming to me again, & the letter could not be sent after him. It will however be the lot of my Brother [George] Hadfield to have this honor. He looks up to you for protection, & trusts in your justice. I can only beg for your indulgence in this instance of double intrusion.

I shall flatter myself with the certainty of your remembrance towards me. Send me few words to assure me I live in your esteem & friendship & you will revive the happiness of ever Yours afly:

Maria Cosway

P.S. I have seen several letters from America which give a most desolate account of the Catholics. Can you be of any use or relief to them? Oh I wish they may find the friend in you that I have found!

God bless you—[27]

Cosway wishes to congratulate Jefferson upon being chosen as the third president of the United States, but she is somewhat tongue-tied. "Words cannot express all I should say on the subject," but she acknowledges that Jefferson can readily read into the emotions behind her words through the use of his abundance of "sympathising sentiment." Does she now think herself to be wholly unworthy of Jefferson's affection, filial or amorous? She then asks

---

[26] "Who has been sincerely devoted to you."
[27] "To Thomas Jefferson from Maria Cosway, 20 July 1801," *Founders Online*, National Archives, https://founders.archives.gov/documents/Jefferson/01-34-02-0458. [Original source: *The Papers of Thomas Jefferson*, vol. 34, *1 May–31 July 1801*, ed. Barbara B. Oberg. Princeton: Princeton University Press, 2007, pp. 599–600.]

Jefferson to look after her brother George, who will be delivering the letter to Jefferson.

Cosway says nothing to Jefferson about the death of her daughter, Louisa Paolina Angelica, on August 6, 1796. Figure 5-3 depicts young Louisa, drawn by her father, in her coffin.[28] Jefferson instead learns of the sad event earlier from exiled Polish patriot Julian Niemcewicz. Jefferson writes to Angelica Church years earlier (11 Jan. 1798):

> We have with us a Mr. Niemcewitz, a Polish gentleman who was with us at Paris when Mrs. Cosway was there and who was of her society in London last summer. He mentions the loss of her daughter, and the gloom into which that and other circumstances has thrown her, that it has taken the hue of religion, that she is solely devoted to religious exercises and superintendent of a school she has instituted for Catholic children, but that she still speaks of her friends here with tenderness and desire. Our letters have been rare but they have let me see that her gayety was gone and her mind entirely placed on the world to come.[29]

Jefferson is preoccupied with politics at this time, so letters to intimates take a back seat to political letters. Nonetheless, his letter to Church intimates another reason for the neglect of his end of their correspondence. The Maria Cosway that he has come to know in Paris is gone. She has become a perpetual penitent. Jefferson has in mind, particularly her philosophical letter of December 4, 1795, in which she begins by the expression of disgust with reality and longing for the afterlife. Jefferson, no believer in an afterlife,[30] can only be much disappointed with Cosway's disgust of life. He is happy for her relegation to domesticity but unhappy with her withdrawal from the world.

It seems clear that Cosway has not been inordinately attached to little Louisa. Yet the child's death, not long after her return, decimates the artist. Had she stayed in London with her daughter after her birth, the child would likely still

---

[28] Cosway merely writes in his autobiographical letter to Sir William Cosway, "She was seized by a sore throat and in the sixth year of her age we lost her." That succinct account is mostly uninformative. Gerald Barnett, *Richard and Maria Cosway: A Biography* (Cambridge: Lutterworth Press, 1995), 261.
[29] "From Thomas Jefferson to Angelica Church, 11 January 1798," *Founders Online*, National Archives, https://founders.archives.gov/documents/Jefferson/01-30-02-0011. [Original source: *The Papers of Thomas Jefferson*, vol. 30, *1 January 1798-31 January 1799*, ed. Barbara B. Oberg. Princeton: Princeton University Press, 2003, pp. 23–24.]
[30] M. Andrew Holowchak, "Jefferson and the Afterlife," *American Messiah: The Surprisingly Simple Religious Views of Thomas Jefferson* (Abilene: Texas Christian University Press, 2019), chap. 4.

be alive. Moreover, Cosway likely takes Louisa's death as a divine omen. Cosway is to mend her profligate ways and live the remainder of her life as a religious ascetic to atone for her profligacy.

**Figure 5-3:** Richard Cosway, Louisa Paolina Cosway on Her Deathbed, 1796

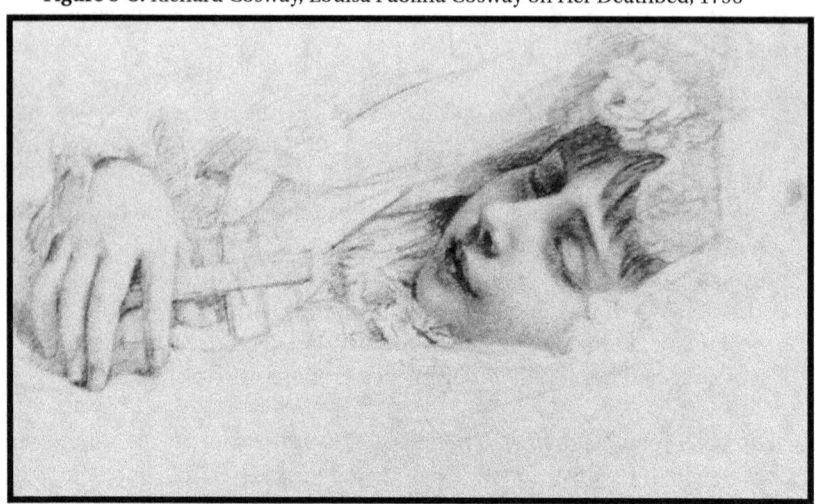

Source: Foundation of Maria Cosway, Lodi, Italy

### "Would it not be a rest for you?"
## MC to TJ, 25 Paris, Feb. 1802, with Enclosure

Dear Sir

I have had the pleasure of writting to you several times, but not that of hearing from you for a long time. Surely you have not forgotten such an old friend! I am now in the place which brings me to mind every day our first interview, the pleasing days we pass'd together. I send you the prospectus of a work which is the most interesting ever published as every body will have in their possession the exact distribution of this wonderfull gallery. The history of every picture will also be very curious as we have collected in one spot the finest works of art which were spread all over Italy.

I hope you will make it known among your friends who may like to know of such a work. This will keep me here two years at least & every body seem very Much delighted with this interprise.

*The Years 1790 to 1805*                                                                 93

Have we hopes of ever seeing you in Paris? would it not be a rest for you after your laborious situation? I often see the only freind remaining of our set, Madme: de Corney, the same in her own amiable qualities but very different in her Situation, but she supports it very well.

I am come to this place in its best time for the profusion of fine things is beyond description & not possible to Conceive. It is so changed in every respect, that you would not think it the same Country or people.

shall this letter be fortunate enough to get to your hands! will it be still More fortunate to procure me an answer! I leave you to reflect on the happiness you will afford your ever afct: & sincere

M Cosway

### GALLERY OF THE LOUVRE, AT PARIS (1st February 1802)

It is proposed to publish by subscription highly finished ETCHINGS, done by Mrs. MARIA COSWAY, of all the PICTURES which compose the superb collection in the gallery of the Louvre, comprising the most celebrated CHEFS-D'OEUVRE of the ITALIAN, FLEMISH, and FRENCH schools; with an historical account of each picture, and such authentic anecdotes of the artists, as may be new and interesting by J. GRIFFITHS, esqre.

The above work will be published by numbers, each containing TWO etchings and the text, printed on superfine paper, with beautiful types; the first number will be ready for delivery on the 31st March next, and if possible, TWO will be given in each future month.

Each place will represent the pictures which compose ONE of the compartments of the gallery, which is at present divided into fifty seven, and the work will be continued until the whole of the collection may be compleated.

The size of the plates is twenty one inches in height by seventeen in breadth, and the TWO first will contain copies of the works of the following masters:

| Raffaello | 7 | Procaccino | 1 |
| Giulio Romano | 5 | Domenico Feti | 1 |
| Tizziano | 4 | Sebastiano del Piombo | 1 |
| Leonardo da Vinci | 2 | Guercino | 1 |
| Paolo Veronese | 2 | Baldassar Peruzzi | 1 |
| Guido | 1 | Alessandro Veronese | 1 |

The numbers will be delivered in strict conformity with the dates of the subscriptions, which it is requested may be paid on receipt of each number.

The impressions will be of two kinds, colored and plain.

| | |
|---|---|
| price to subscribers, | |
| For each number, with two colored etchings, | L 1–, 5– |
| Do., with two plain, | 15– |
| price to non-subscribers, | |
| For each number, with two colored etchings, | L 1–, 11–, 6– |
| Do., with two plain, | 1–, 1– |

Subscribers, a list of whom will be given with the work, are sollicited to signify their intentions to M. COLNAGHI, Cockspur street, LONDON, who will carefully direct the numbers according to order, grant receipts for the amount of subscriptions paid (if required), and with whom may be seen a specimen of the etchings.[31]

Jefferson replies over 11 months later and essays to address Cosway's concerns from her last two letters.

### "An attachment which has never been diminished"
### TJ to MC, Washington, 31 Jan. 1803

My dear friend

I have to acknolege the reciept of your favor of July 20. 1801. from London, and of Feb. 25. 1802. from Paris. that I am so late in answering them arises from my incessant occupations which deprive me of the happiness of satisfying the affections of my heart by expressions of them on paper to my friends: to none would they be more warmly expressed, my esteemed friend, than to yourself, with whom the first interview produced an attachment which has never been diminished.

---

[31] "Enclosure: Proposal to Publish Etchings of Pictures in the Louvre, 1 February 1802," *Founders Online*, National Archives, https://founders.archives.gov/documents/Jefferson/01-36-02-0421-0002. [Original source: *The Papers of Thomas Jefferson*, vol. 36, *1 December 1801–3 March 1802*, ed. Barbara B. Oberg. Princeton: Princeton University Press, 2009, p. 637.]

and you are now at Paris, enjoying the remains of our friends there, basking in all the varieties of happiness which that place yields, indulging your taste & talents for painting and preparing to treat the world with a representation of the splendid works you are feasting on yourself. a splendid work yours will be, I am sure, and I wished long ago to have said so to you, and to have asked you to set me down as a subscriber. I see by the prospectus that the numbers are to be delivered & paid for in London, and shall take measures accordingly. this will be carried by my best friend mr Monroe, who is sent to Paris on an occasional diplomatic mission. he is the honestest man alive, and carries with him, in mrs Monroe, a specimen of our American beauties. any letter you may at any time confide to him for me will be safely forwarded; and besides wishing to learn the progress you make in your work, I am always wishing to hear of your health and happiness.

you express anxieties for the catholic religion here. all religions here are equally free, and equally protected by the laws, and left to be supported by their own respective votaries. in some places the Catholic is better off than other sects, as they possess valuable endowments of land.

your brother is well. he has lately superintended the erection of a public building with entire approbation. cherish on your part the friendship of our former days, and be assured of my constant and sincere affection & respect.

Th: Jefferson[32]

Jefferson must be elated by the contents of Cosway's letter of 1802, which, unlike the letter from 1801, shows some spark of vitality. Cosway is returning to her work and is to copy and craft etchings of all the great works at the Louvre—a project of immense difficulty and requiring intense focus of time. The aim is to etch onto copper plates each of the pictures of the Grand Gallery. Subscribers will get two plates each month, and the project will be completed in two and a half years. Cosway has gained subscriptions from Josephine Bonapartes, Lucien Bonaparte, the Prince of Wales, Duke of Cumberland, and Earl Cowper, and so the project is no will-o'-the-wisp.

While still in Paris in 1802, Cosway will make the acquaintance of Joseph Fesch (1763–1839, Figure 5-4), an uncle of Napoleon Bonaparte. Fesch will become a dear friend and one who likely falls for Cosway.[33] Fesch will become

---

[32] "From Thomas Jefferson to Maria Cosway, 31 January 1803," *Founders Online*, National Archives, https://founders.archives.gov/documents/Jefferson/01-39-02-0360. [Original source: *The Papers of Thomas Jefferson*, vol. 39, *13 November 1802–3 March 1803*, ed. Barbara B. Oberg. Princeton: Princeton University Press, 2012, pp. 418–419.]

[33] Gerald Barnett, *Richard and Maria Cosway*, 160.

archbishop and soon cardinal, and the two will often discuss Catholic education. The cardinal convinces Cosway to found a Catholic school for girls in Lyon. She does in 1805.[34]

**Figure 5-4:** Cardinal Joseph Fesch, n.d.

Source: Wikipedia Commons

Gerald Barnett writes of Cosway's turn of mind at this juncture of her life. At the loss of Louisa, "a smothered melancholy corroded her heart," and she "at different times displayed somewhat like a carelessness of existence." She is amused by Paris but looks upon the mirabilia of the Louvre with "sated eye."

> The business of life seemed to be the pursuit of pleasure. The couch of voluptuousness lay under a bower of roses. Beauty sported her unveiled graces before her sight; and her bright copies, shining in Parian marble, retreatd amid the foliage of a thousand groves, in envy of the fairer original. From such scenes of more than eastern luxury, Maria Cosway resolved to withdraw.[35]

---

[34] For more, see "The Artist," *Foundazione Maria Cosway,* http://www.fondazionemariacosway.it/en/artist.html, accessed 8 Sept. 2022.
[35] Gerald Barnett, *Richard and Maria Cosway,* 160.

During the first year of Jefferson's second term as president of the United States, Cosway again writes Jefferson from her school at Lyons. There will be a gap of over 13 years before the next letter in the correspondence, again penned by Cosway.

### "Time goes apace with distance"
## MC to TJ, Lyons, 10 Oct. 1805

It is very difficult to give up some friends, tho' time goes apace with distance. We cannot forget those we have once highly esteemed. It is to seldom I have an opportunity of enquiring whether I am forgotten tho' the reasons are not the same to be remembered.

The brother of a Lady who lives with me, Mr. Philippe is going to America and I have asked him to take this short letter [with hope that it will be] received at least with half the pleasure [it is] written.

Here I have been two years & my establishment goes on extremely well & have the consolation of being Mother of 60 children. Nothing is more interesting than rendring oneself usefull to our fellow creatures, & what better way than that of managing their education.

What is become of my Brother [George] he never writes to any of his family. I have however teken every opportunity to write to him.

Believe me dear Sir, ever the same most affecte & obliged

M. Cosway[36]

Cosway's sentiment—"Nothing is more interesting than rendering oneself useful to our fellow creatures, & what better way than that of managing their education"—could have been penned by Jefferson, as it is a sentiment commonly seen in his letters, especially to his daughters. Is Cosway, by this time, longing lovingly for Jefferson?

Fesch will become archbishop of Lyon, and the war between France and England will make it difficult to maintain her school. Calumny will follow Cosway. Abbé Goullard and the nuns of the school will force her removal from the institution. The sisters have in mind more the preservation of their order

---

[36] "Maria Cosway to Thomas Jefferson, 7 April 1819," *Founders Online*, National Archives, https://founders.archives.gov/documents/Jefferson/03-14-02-0196. [Original source: *The Papers of Thomas Jefferson*, Retirement Series, vol. 14, *1 February to 31 August 1819*, ed. J. Jefferson Looney. Princeton: Princeton University Press, 2017, pp. 207–209.]

than an above-board educational institution in the service of bettering the lives of its students.[37]

---

[37] Carol Burnell, *Divided Affections*, 360–62, and Gerald Barnett, *Richard and Maria Cosway*, 163.

Chapter VI

# The Years 1819 to 1824

Beginning with a letter from Maria Cosway after a lengthy respite in their correspondence, there will be seven more letters between the two: Cosway penning five; Jefferson, two.

True to Jefferson's assessment, the years from 1805 to her death on January 5, 1838, are ascetic, penitential. Cosway's focus will be to be "usefull" by opening a Catholic school for girls. There are significant deaths: her dear friend Gen. Pasquale Paoli in 1807; her mother, Isabella, in 1810; Francesco Melzi d'Eril, Duke of Lodi, in 1816; Cosway's sister Elisabetta in 1820; and her husband, Richard, in 1821 at their new residence at 31 Edgware Road—"a very tiny but cosy house." Prior to his death, Richard will become increasingly eccentric, drawn to the occult, and increasingly living in an imagined reality.[1] In 1811, Maria Cosway, with the aid of the Duke of Lodi, founded in Lodi her Collegia de Beata Vergine delle Grazie. Cosway moves to Lodi on February 18, 1812. Her friend Francesco Melzi d'Eril (1753–1816) purchases the Monastry of the Minimi Friars to become Cosway's school, which opens on April 2 and has 42 students later in the same year.

Jefferson will be engaged in a number of significant projects. After his tense second term as president, he will, following Washington's lead, retire and leave the presidency in the hands of his secretary of state, James Madison. Jefferson's immediate focus will be his massively rundown plantation, but he will soon devolve its management over to his grandson, Thomas Jefferson Randolph, and turn his attention to a prominent educational institution in Virginia that will morph into the University of Virginia. The cornerstone of Pavilion VII is laid in 1817. Still saddled heavily with debt, Jefferson's fiscal ruination is sealed when close friend Wilson Cary Nicholas asks for Jefferson's signature on a 20,000-dollar loan. Nicholas dies the next year, and Jefferson will assume the massive debt. University of Virginia (Figure 6-1) formally opens on March 7, 1825. Jefferson, along with dear friend John Adams, will die on July 4, 1826—the fiftieth anniversary of Declaration of Independence.

---

[1] Gerald Barnett, *Richard and Maria Cosway: A Biography* (Cambridge: Lutterworht Press, 1995), 190.

**Figure 6-1:** C. Bohn, *University of Virginia*, 1856

Source: Library Of Congress Online.

After a respite of over 13 years, Cosway breaks the long silence between the two.

## "It has afforded me Satisfactions Unfelt before"
## MC to TJ, London, 7 Apr. 1819

Dear Sir

You must allow that all those who have had the happiness of your Acquaintance, will ever remember its value. Those, Still farther favoured by a Correspondence have a constant Satisfaction of reading over your Sentiments, your heart, all in Short that can imprint everlasting acknowledgements of esteem, Admiration, freindship & gratitude. What share I must possess of all these, I leave you to judge, & hope that neither time Nor distance will ever bring me to your recolection as importune. Tho farr from deserving any degree of those qualifications ascribed to you above, you will I hope admit the Second part belonging to me.

A favorable oportunity offers itself to me of writting to you, can I resist it?

To the lenght of Silence I draw a Curtain. Remembrance must be ever Green. Circumstances have been too evident, to want Any justification for the interuption of corresponding. Sufice it to Say that the mind has not had a moment's part in it[2]

Was there not So great a distance between us, I should end My letter here, but to break off while there might be a probability of Some interrogation, Such as, "What have you been about all this while? Where have you been"? &c.

If I may presume Some freindly wish of this kind probable, I must proceed, & plead indulgence for your reading me longer. Often have I read your name in the papers, therefore have been Acquainted of your proceedings in that honorable way which was expected from you.

My humble Situation Could never bring to you Any public informations of me, & I little trust on private ones being built on Truth.

My different journies on the Continent were either forced by bad health, or other particular private Maloncholy Motives: but On Any Sudden information of M$^r$ C's bad health, I hastend home; to See him.

In my stay on the Continent I was call'd to form Establishments of Education, one at Lyons which met with the most flattering Success. And lastly one in Italy, equaly Answering every hoped for Consolation. Oh! how often have I thought of America! wished to have exerted myself there. Who would have imagined, I should have taken up this line? it has afforded me Satisfactions Unfelt before; After having been deprived of my own child.

what Confortable feelings, Seeing children grow up accomplishd, modest, & virtuos Women! They hardly are gone home from the Establishment at fifteen, but Are married & become paterns to their Sexe.

But Am I not breaking the rules of Modesty myself, & boast too Much? in what better manner can I relate this? However, tho Seeminly Settled at Lodi, my duties were ever ready to return home when call'd.

At last, at the first Opening of a Comunication at the cessation of the cruel hostilities which kept us all assunder, alarm'd at the indiferent occounts of M[r.]$^r$ C's state of health, I hastend home. He is much broke, & has had two paralitik stroeks, the last of which has deprived him of the use of his wright hand & arm.

Forgotten by the Arts, Suspended the direction of education (tho it is going on vastly well in my Absence) I am now excercising the occupations of a Nurse. Happy in Self gratification of doing my duty, with no other consolation. In Your

---

[2] It is all Heart; there is no Head in this.

Dialogue your head would tell me, "that is enough," your heart perhaps will understand, I might wish for more. God's will be done.

What a loss to me not having the beloved M^rs Church! And how greved I was when told she was no more Among the living.

I used to See Madame de Corny at Paris, she Still lives but in bad health. that is the only one of our Common friends we knew. Strange changes over & over again all Over Europe.

You only are proceeding on well.

Now, my dear Sir, forgive this long letter, may I flatter myself to hear from you? give me Some occount of yourself as you used to do, instead of Challiou & Paris taulk to me of Monticello. &.

Accept of the best wishes from One, who, ever retains with the deepest Sense of gratitude your kindness to her & wishes most Ardently to find a place in your remembrance as one who ever will be Yours most Sincerely & aff^ly

Maria Cosway

P.S. I wrote a letter not long ago to M^r Trumble, I hope he will Send me An Answer, I have Never heard from my brother.[3]

---

Cosway writes of her "private Melancholy Motives." At some point, she is called "to form Establishments of Education," first at Lyons and then at Lodi, and "equally Answering every hoped for Consolation."

What is the consolation about which Cosway speaks?

It is the consolation of devoting the remainder of her life to being a mother to many young girls after the death of her own girl and of being a nurse to her debilitated husband. In her words, "Happy in Self-gratification of doing my duty, with no other consolation." That is sufficient, as Jefferson's Head might say, though Heart might pine for more. Cosway can never overcome the guilt she certainly feels about the death of her young daughter after she has spent the first four years away from the child. She is, in her mind, the cause of young Louisa's death, whose passing is a warning of the Virgin Mother for Cosway to mend her ways or to suffer eternal damnation. Failure to be a mother to her daughter she is to be a mother to numerous other young girls and to direct their thoughts to modesty and virtue.

---

[3] "Maria Cosway to Thomas Jefferson, 7 April 1819," *Founders Online,* National Archives, https://founders.archives.gov/documents/Jefferson/03-14-02-0196. [Original source: *The Papers of Thomas Jefferson,* Retirement Series, vol. 14, *1 February to 31 August 1819,* ed. J. Jefferson Looney. Princeton: Princeton University Press, 2017, pp. 207–209.]

In addition to the "Consolation," there are certain "Satisfactions," which revolve around thoughts of being in America to exert herself there and without question with Jefferson.

Cosway asks for a reply, but not a mawkish letter that talks of the years in France. She wants to hear of Monticello.

Although Jefferson does not reply for well over a year, there is little reason to question that he receives Cosway's letter after so many years passed with great relish. He replies just after Christmas in 1820. It is likely again the Christmas season, dear to Catholics, that brings to mind Cosway.

### "I have never lost sight of your letter"
## TJ to MC, Monticello, 27 Dec. 1820

'Over the length of silence I draw a curtain,' is an expression, my dear friend, of your cherished letter of Apr. 7. 19. of which, it might seem, I have need to avail myself; but not so really. to 77. heavy years add two of prostrate health during which all correspondence has been suspended of necessity, and you have the true cause of not having heard from me. my wrist too, dislocated in Paris while I had the pleasure of being there with you, is, by the effect of years, now so stiffened, that writing is become a most slow and painful operation, and scarcely ever undertaken but under the goad of imperious business. but I have never lost sight of your letter, and give it now the first place among those of my transatlantic friends which have been laying unacknoleged during the same period of ill health.

I rejoice in the first place that you are well; for your silence on that subject encorages me to presume it. and next that you have been so usefully and pleasingly occupied in preparing the minds of others to enjoy the blessings you have yourself derived from the same source, a cultivated mind. of mr Cosway I fear to say any thing, such is the disheartening account of the state of his health given in your letter. but here or wherever, I am sure he has all the happiness which an honest life ensures. nor will I say any thing of the troubles of those among whom you live. I see they are grea[t] and wish them happily out of them, and especially that you may be safe and happy, whatever be their issue.

I will talk about Monticello then, and my own country, as is the wish expressed in your letter. my daughter Randolph whom you knew in Paris a young girl, is now the mother of 11. living children, the grandmother of about half a dozen others, enjoys health and good spirits and sees the worth of her husband attested by his being at present Governor of the state in which we live. among these I live, like a patriarch of old. our friend Trumbull is well, &

profitably & honorably employed by his country in commemorating with his pencil some of it's revolutionary honors. of mrs Cruger I hear nothing, nor, for a long time, of Mad$^e$ de Corny. such is the present state of our former coterie, dead, diseased & dispersed. but "tout ce qui est différé n'est pas perdu,"[4] says the French proverb, and the religion you so sincerely profess, tells us we shall meet again, and we have all so lived as to be assured it will be in happiness.

mine is the next turn, and I shall meet it with good will. for after one's friends are all gone before them, and our faculties leaving us too, one by one, why wish to linger in mere vegetation? as a solitary trunk in a desolate field, from which all it's former companions have disappeared. you have many good years remaining yet to be happy yourself and to make those around you happy. may these, my dear friend, be as many as yourself may wish, and all of them filled with health and happiness will be among the last & warmest wishes of an unchangeable friend.

Th: Jefferson[5]

Jefferson cites ill health in his "heavy years" for failure to write Cosway but has placed her missive at the top of a heap of unanswered letters by "transatlantic friends." That, it must be noted, is a qualification. She is no longer first among all others but first among Transatlantic friends.

Sweeping over the other concerns, as Cosway bids, Jefferson agrees to focus on the affairs of his life at Monticello, and he does. It is a warm and friendly letter from a man whose best years are far behind him and yet who is ready to greet death with "good will." He wishes sincerely that Cosway's remaining years are industrious and happy—the latter implying the former—and he senses, wrongly, that she is now happy.

Over six months later, Cosway writes to Jefferson to relate that her husband, Richard Cosway, has passed from a third apoplectic fit.

---

[4] "All things different are not lost."
[5] "Thomas Jefferson to Maria Cosway, 27 December 1820," *Founders Online*, National Archives, https://founders.archives.gov/documents/Jefferson/03-16-02-0403. [Original source: *The Papers of Thomas Jefferson*, Retirement Series, vol. 16, *1 June 1820 to 28 February 1821*, ed. J. Jefferson Looney et al. Princeton: Princeton University Press, 2019, pp. 497–499.]

### "I have been left a *widow*"
## MC to TJ, 15 July 1821

My dear & most esteem'd friend

The Appearance of this letter will inform you that I have been left a *widow*. Poor Mr. Cosway was suddenly taken by an Apoplective fit—and being the *third* proved this *last*. At the time we had hoped he would enjoy a few years—for he never had been so well & happy—the change of air was found necessary to his health; I took a very charming house & fitted it up handsome & comfortable, with those pictures & things he like most. All my thoughts and actions were for him.

He had neglected his affairs very much and when I was obliged to make them in my hands was astonished. I took every means to ammelliorate them & had succeeded, at last for his Comforts. And my Consolation was his contantly repeating how *well* & how *hapy* he was.

We had an auction of all his affects & house in Stratoford Place, which lasted two months. My fatigue has been excessive,—the sale did not produce as much as we expected, but enough to make him comfortable & free from embarrassment, as he might have been if I had not acted accordingly. Every body thought he was very rich & I was astonished when put to the *real* knowledge of his situation.

He made his will two years ago, & left me to be his executrix & mistress of every thing. After having settled every things here & provided for three Cousins of Mr. C's I shall retire fro[m] this bustling & *insignificant* world, to my favorite College at Lodi as I always intended, where I can employ myself so happily in doing good.

I wish *Monticello* was not *so far!* I would pay you a visit if it was [not] ever so much out of my way, but it is impossible.

I long to hear from you—the remembrance of a person I so highly esteem & venerate, affords me the happiest consolation & your *Patriarcal* situation delights me. Such as I expected from you.

Notwithstanding your indifference for a World you make one of the most distinguished members & ornament, I wish you may still enjoy many years & feel the happiness of the Nation which produces such Caracters.

I will write again before I leave this Country at this moment in so boisterous as occupation as you must be inform'd of—& I will send you my direction. I shall pass thro' Paris & taulk of you with Madame de Corny. Believe me every your most affte & obliged

Maria Cosway

P.S. I hope you will forgive the liberty I take of enclosing a letter from my Brother as I think it will be the more safely delivered to him.⁶

The letter finds Cosway, who has been nursing her moribund husband, arranging her affairs so that she might leave London for Lodi. Her school takes the place of retirement to a convent, for there she can "retire fro[m] this bustling & *insignificant* world" and again following Jefferson's prescription for happiness, "where I can employ myself so happily in doing good."

It is very noteworthy that Cosway immediately adds her thwarted desire to visit Jefferson—the desire thwarted because of the immense distance, but also, though unstated, the parlousness of such a journey for a woman, especially one of advancing age. It is probable that if there were some way for them to be together, she would prefer that to the cloister of the school. Yet as she says in her letter of April 7, 1819, "God's will be done"—that is, "God probably does not see fit for that to happen." Cosway must pay the price for her profligacy and retire to a life of industry and virtue. Used throughout her life to being around *bon vivants*, flatterers especially, it is not a happy prospect for her.

That becomes abundantly manifest in her next missive to Jefferson, another heavily philosophical letter, over a year after her last.

### "All in trouble, all at work, for what!"

## MC to TJ, London, 10 July 1822

My dear friend

I have at last finished all the affairs which have kept me here after the loss of poor Mʳ Cosway and am returning to the tranquillity, good climate & favorite as well as usefull occupation of my dear College at Lodis. I promised in my last to acquaint you of my destination that I might have the pleasure of hearing from you, little did I expect I should be detain so long.

In appearance Mʳ C. passed for being very rich, but in reality was far from it, little had but what depended on the Sale of his valuable & immense Collection & that sold for very little, the times are bad here, all complain for want of money, and it is too natural every one will deprive themselves of the Superfluos, and only in that the Colection Consisted, However, if what I have is not Sufficient

---

⁶ "Maria Cosway to Thomas Jefferson, 15 July 1821," *Founders Online,* National Archives, https://founders.archives.gov/documents/Jefferson/03-17-02-0303. [Original source: *The Papers of Thomas Jefferson,* Retirement Series, vol. 17, *1 March to 30 November 1821,* ed. J. Jefferson Looney et al. Princeton: Princeton University Press, 2020, pp. 282–283.]

for this Country where I am going I shall be Comfortable and at ease. My activity requires some occupation & what I have chosen is a glorious one, & every Circumstance does incourage me to it, particularly its happy Success. I have lost many valuable old friends and at my Age & my sentiments new ones I little care for. Children are growing tender plants, & by planting virtues in their hearts & minds, affection & gratitude reward & console my assiduity & labours, and is a Constant Succession of Satisfaction & enjoiment.

But, as this is about my self; permit me to be anxious about you, & to enquire the state of your health, happy you will ever be, because you know too well in what best happiness Consists, after all it much depends on the choice we make; & in what we make it Consist, and yours must be Successfull.

The whole world is a good lesson, all in trouble, all at work, for what! in constant ambitious Struggles, aiming at impossibility to obtain, & end on a road in the middle of the Seas.

I wish I could see you, or your charming Monticello! Could I drop back some of my years I should be happy to pay you a Visit. I have visited Scotland & have been delighted, the Scenery beautifull & the nation brave; Constant & faithfull to the Sentiments of their forefathers of whom they inherit the characteristic Virtues. How *this* nation triffles itself away!

I hope to hear from you, a letter addressed to Lodi via Milan will find your ever obliged & sincerely aff^te

Maria Cosway

I beg to be remembered to your daughter. Can you tell me where my brother (George Hadfield) is, & what he is about?[7]

Cosway gripes about the contentiousness of humans—"constant ambitious Struggles, aiming at impossibility to obtain, & end on the road in the middle of the Seas." The letter to Jefferson is Cosway's confession of lifelong sinning, impossible to eschew in a tumultuous world. Jefferson, who knows "too well in what best happiness Consists," is her confessor.

It is again to be noted that after the proclamation of the futility of striving for gain, she immediately expresses a wish to see Jefferson.

---

[7] "Maria Cosway to Thomas Jefferson, 10 July 1822," *Founders Online,* National Archives, https://founders.archives.gov/documents/Jefferson/03-18-02-0475. [Original source: *The Papers of Thomas Jefferson,* Retirement Series, vol. 18, *1 December 1821 to 15 September 1822,* ed. J. Jefferson Looney et al. Princeton: Princeton University Press, 2021, pp. 536–537.]

Jefferson, perhaps sensing Cosway's disconsolation, replies only after some three months.

### "The sympathies of our early days harmonise"
### TJ to MC, Monticello, 24 Oct. 1822

I duly recieved, my dear friend, your favor of July 10. and made it my first duty to forward the letter you inclosed to your brother and to request him to make me the channel of your hearing from him. I now inclose you his letter, and with it the assurance that he is much respected in Washington, and, since the death of Latrobe, our first Architect, I consider him as standing foremost in the correct principles of that art. I believe he is doing well, but would he push himself more, he would do better.

I learn with great pleasure that however short of expectation mr Cosway's affairs left you, they are still sufficient to place you in comfort. and this will be much improved by the change of your residence from the eternal clouds and rains of England, to the genial sun & bright skies of Lodi. I was in that place in 1786. with a good friend, the Count del Verme of Milan. and past a whole day, from sunrise to sunset, in a dairy there, [...] to see the process of making the Parmesan cheese. it's situation is truly wise of your choice.

The sympathies of our earlier days harmonise, it seems in age also. you retire to your College of Lodi, and nourish the natural benevolence of your excellent heart by communicating your own virtues to the young of your sex who may hereafter load with blessings the memory of her to whom they will owe so much. I, am laying the foundation of an University in my native state, which I hope will repay the liberalities of it's legislature by improving the virtue and science of their country, already blest with a soil and climate emulating those of your favorite Lodi. I have been myself the Architect of the plan of it's buildings, and of it's system of instruction. four years have been employed on the former, and I assure you it would be thought a handsome & Classical thing in Italy. I have preferred the plan of an Academical village rather than that of a single, massive structure. the diversified forms which this admitted in the different Pavilions, and varieties of the finest samples of architecture, has made of it a model of beauty original and unique. it is within view too of Monticello, So it's most splendid object, and a constant gratification to my sight. we have still one building to erect, which will be on the principle of your Pantheon a Rotunda like that, but of half it's diameter and height only. I wish indeed you could recall some of your by-past years and seal it with your approbation.

you have two friends here, still living, Trumbull & myself to whom such a visit would be real beatitude.

I enjoy good health, altho now octogenary; but am too week to walk further than my garden; but I ride daily and without fatigue. my elder daughter, mrs Randolph, [...] and greets you kindly. she has given me 11. grand-children, of whom 9. live with me, and all make me contented in the prospect of the [...] worth and good qualifications. my happiness is greatly increased too by the prosperity of our country, and it's exemption from the oppressions & eternal wars of Europe.

that your days may pass in peace, in health and comfort are the fervent prayers of your sincere & constant friend.

Th: Jefferson[8]

Jefferson begins with some kind words concerning Cosway's brother, George, but he then adds, "The sympathies of our earlier days harmonise, it seems in age also." While Cosway retires to her school in Lodi, Jefferson is "laying the foundation of an University" in Virginia. He dilates on his role not only in founding the University of Virginia but also in its design and construction. There is some soft encouragement for Cosway to visit him and Trumbull; his decrepitude, he implicitly says, prevents him from visiting her.

Jefferson is wholly impervious to Cosway's pleas in her last four letters that the two should again see each other. There seems to be by Cosway a pithily expressed but desperate longing for Jefferson in those letters. Jefferson merely assumes that she, now gainfully industrious, must be happy. Yet Cosway is merely following Jefferson's blueprint for happiness, but actions in conformancy with virtue without a virtuous disposition cannot lead to tranquility. Cosway, ever doomed to the antipodes of profligacy and penitency, will ever be miserable. The right thing to do without choice and without a virtuous disposition is not virtuous activity.[9] Cosway is deedy merely from compunction and from a need to pass her days, not from a settled disposition to industry.

Cosway replies some eight months later to Jefferson's missive.

---

[8] "Maria Cosway to Thomas Jefferson, 10 July 1822," *Founders Online*, National Archives, https://founders.archives.gov/documents/Jefferson/03-18-02-0475. [Original source: *The Papers of Thomas Jefferson*, Retirement Series, vol. 18, *1 December 1821 to 15 September 1822*, ed. J. Jefferson Looney et al. Princeton: Princeton University Press, 2021, pp. 536–537.]

[9] Aristotle for instance in Book II.4 of *Nichomachean Ethics* states that an action is virtuous if and only if the agent knows that it is the right thing to do, he deliberately chooses that action, and he acts from settled (virtuous) disposition. Aristotle, *Nicomachean Ethics*, trans. H. Rackham (Cambridge: Harvard University Press [1926] 1990), Book II.4.

## "That immense Sea, Makes it a great distance"
## MC to TJ, Milan, 18 June 1823

Dear Sir

As I have found a favorable oportunity of Conveing a letter, I am happy to profit of it, to thank you for Good & friendly letter which I received at Lodi. I congratulate you in the undertaking you Announceme[nt] of the fine building which occupies your taste & knowledge, & gratifies your heart, the work is worthy of you, you be worthy of such enjoyment Nothing, I think, is more usefull to Mankind than a good Education. I may say have been very fortunate to give a Spring to it in this Country & See those Children I have had the care of turn out good Wives, excellent Mothers, et bonnes femmes d Manage, which was not understood in those Countries, and which is the principle object of Society and the only usefull. I wish I could come & <u>learn</u> from you; was it the furthest part of Europe Nothing would prevent me. but that immense Sea, Makes it a great distance. I hope however to hear from you as often as you can favor me.

I am glad you approve my choice of Lodi, it is a quite lovely place, & far from the bugel [bungle?] of the world which is become trublesome.

what a change since you was here! I saw Mad. De Corny when at Paris, she is the Same only a little older, but well, we taulk'd of you.

I know well all the family Del Verenzo & her two Children in my establishment, one is just going to be married to one of the first Nobleman here.

I take the liberty to send another letter to my Brother, I [am] glad to hear he goes on well, & know he does not find himself forward, this is a family fault I recomend him to you in what you Can be of use to him. Since diffidence is his only fault.

I beg to be rememberd to M$^r$: Trumbull.

Believe me, my good friend, Your most aff$^t$, obliged

Maria Cosway[10]

There is again in this letter the articulated desire to see Jefferson—this time, avowedly, to learn from him. The intimation is that she wishes to learn about running a school, but I suspect that that is merely the proximate or stated goal. In the letter to Jefferson of July 10, 1822, Cosway concedes that Jefferson knows

---

[10] "To Thomas Jefferson from Maria Hadfield Cosway, 18 June 1823," *Founders Online*, National Archives, https://founders.archives.gov/documents/Jefferson/98-01-02-3580. [This is an **Early Access document** from The Papers of Thomas Jefferson: Retirement Series.

what is likely to be the riddle of life: how to be happy. Cosway is elliptically telling Jefferson that she is dreadfully unhappy. Jefferson, trying to deal with his pecuniary problems, is either unmindful of her fairly obvious hints or neglectful of them, for at this point, he has familial obligations, and he cannot disregard his family to attend to her needs. Whereas Cosway fails to requite Jefferson's love of her early in their relationship, Cosway, now alone in the world and in desperate need of Jefferson, finds her correspondent unresponsive.

Fifteen months later, Cosway writes the last known letter in their correspondence. Cosway has returned to Florence for a visit. There is, in this final letter, no mention of wishing to see Jefferson.

### "I have left a hill barren, as I would place Monticello, & the Seminary"
## MC to TJ, Florence, 24 Sept. 1824

My dear Sir & good friend

I am come to visit My Native Country, & am Much delighted with every thing around it. The Arts have Made great progress, and M$^r$ Cosway's Drawings have been Very Much admired, which induced me to place in the Gallery a very fine Portrait of his. I have found here an Opportunity of Sending this letter by Leghorn, which I had not at Milan.

I wish much to hear from you, & how you go on with your fine Seminary. I have had my great Saloon [sic] painted, with the representation of the [various] parts of the world & the most distinguished objects in them I have at a loss for America, as I found very few small prints—however Washington town is marb$^d$ & I have left a hill barren, as I would place Monticello, & the Seminary; if you favor me with some description that I might have it introduced You would Oblige me Much.[11] I am just setting out for my home, pray write to me at Lodi & if this reaches you <u>safe</u> I will write longer by the Same way. Believe me ever

Your Most Oblg$^d$ & aff$^{te}$: friend

Maria Cosway[12]

---

[11] A letter in 1826 from the journal of the wife of art dealer Paul Clanaghi writes of her visit to Cosway's school. She mentions the school's painted walls. "The walls of the ball-room representing the four quarters of the globe." She says nothing of the representation being unfinished. George Charles Williamson, *Richard Cosway, R.A.* (London: George Bell and Sons, 1905), 80.

[12] "To Thomas Jefferson from Maria Hadfield Cosway, 24 September 1824," *Founders Online,* National Archives, https://founders.archives.gov/documents/Jefferson/98-01-02-4563. [This is an **Early Access document** from The Papers of Thomas Jefferson: Retirement Series.

Jefferson never replies. Hellen Bullock merely says, "No opportunity offered for an answer."[13] Carol Burnell maintains that "Jefferson's last illness prevented his replying to her request."[14] He is infirm and preoccupied with his suffocating debt. Nonetheless, it is somewhat astonishing that Jefferson does not drop other concerns, even his debt, to craft a reply and offer some description of Monticello and the University of Virginia for his dear trans-Atlantic friend so she can complete the painting. She can improvise or request some description from the numerous others who have visited Monticello, but she desires that that description come from Jefferson—only from Jefferson.

Cosway leaves the hill, upon which Jefferson's vaunted Monticello sits, barren. She likely, given the obtuseness of her "most sincere & constant friend," thinks it best to leave it that way. The incompleteness of the painting corresponds to the incompleteness of her life.

---

[13] Helen Duprey Bullock, *My Head and My Heart: A Little History of Thomas Jefferson and Maria Cosway* (New York: G.P. Putnam's Sons, 1945), 187.
[14] Carol Burnell, *Divided Affections: The Extraordinary Life of Maria Cosway: Celebrity Artist and Thomas Jefferson's Impossible Love* (London: Column House, 2007), 397.

# Postscript

The love affair between Cosway and Jefferson, if my account is correct, is much more complex than scholars have noted. It is not an account of reciprocated love between two persons that cannot be consummated because of the exigencies of circumstances. It is an account of unreciprocated love early in their relationship—Jefferson's love of Cosway is unrequited—and unreciprocated love late in their relationship—Cosway's love of Jefferson is unrequited.

As is his wont with women with whom he is attracted, Jefferson begins gushingly and volubly his relationship with Cosway. His effusiveness, I argue, frightens Cosway and places her in a defensive posture in the earliest years of their relationship. She welcomes Jefferson's attention—she even demands it—but only from afar and on her terms, and that is how it is with other men in her coterie. Jefferson is her friend, though she grants that he is in the small circle of her most intimate friends.

Cosway's chilliness in those early years—one needs merely to consider her off-putting reply to his *billet doux* when she gives it her fullest attention—gradually attenuates his affection for her. By July 30, 1788, Jefferson is broken. There can be nothing between the two of them. He will settle into the businesses of advancing the interests of his jejune country and of promoting the principles of republican government as well as, years later, of attending to the interests of his daughter Martha and his flock of grandchildren.

Cosway, throughout her long and tortuous life, is ever pulled toward and, thus, riven by the antipodes of profligacy and penitency—the result of early exposure to the festivities in her father's inns and the quiet reclusiveness of her time as a young girl in the convent. Lured by the delights of hedonism, her Catholic conscience, bolstered by her early years with Violante Cerrotti, requires penitence for peace of mind—if only for a time. Cosway is ever challenged and by the shifting demands of life, and by the time of the death of her husband, she too is mostly, if not fully, broken by them. In all her letters except the last since the resumption of her correspondence with Jefferson in 1819, she articulates unequivocally a wish to see Jefferson. The coquette has died and her wish is sincere. Her final years are fraught with compunction. She longs for Jefferson.

Jefferson, saddled by prodigious debt and illness of health, seems oblivious to her wish, and late in life expresses no desire to see again Cosway. Cosway has settled into her school at Lodi, where she can repent for her many sins, especially the death of her daughter, and assume the roles of mother and perhaps confessor to the school's many young girls. She has taken on at the school a wholly domestic role and is thus now a suitable companion for her longtime longanimous suitor, who perpetually advocates that happiness lies in virtuous utility and that virtuous activity for a woman is willful assumption of a domestic role.

Late in life, Cosway longs achingly to see Jefferson. It is she who now irrevocably loves him, though it is no lustful love. She longs to live out the remaining years of her life with him, but recognizes that that cannot happen. Still, if she cannot be with him, she can act like him—virtuously and industriously (e.g., TJ to Maria Cosway, 27 Dec. 1820). Emulation is perhaps the greatest expression of the trueness of her love.

It is heart-rending that Jefferson does not reply to Cosway's final letter—that in her depiction of America in her painting on the school's salon, there will be gaps where Monticello and University of Virginia should be. That, however, is somehow fitting. The gap in her picture of America will be for Cosway a constant reminder in her remaining years that her love for Jefferson goes unrequited, just as his ailing right wrist will be for Jefferson a constant reminder in the early years of their relationship that his love for Cosway goes unrequited.

www.ingramcontent.com/pod-product-compliance
Lightning Source LLC
Chambersburg PA
CBHW051527230426
43668CB00012B/1769